A Dream-Guided Meditation Model and the Personalized Method for Interpreting Dreams

A Dream-Guided Meditation Model and the Personalized Method for Interpreting Dreams presents a model for meditation that counselors can use with clients regardless of gender, race, national origin, religion, age, or marital status. Using the model, readers can, if they wish, learn to interpret nighttime dreams. Even readers who choose not to learn to interpret their dreams may find that the meditation model assists with dream guidance.

Evelyn M. Duesbury, MS Counselor Education, teaches by writing about use of her researched and award-winning Personalized Method for Interpreting Dreams (PMID). Duesbury's American Counseling Association (ACA) credentials include distance credentialed counselor, licensed professional counselor, and continuing education provider. Topics covered in her published works include relationships, counseling, writing, and meditation.

Other Books by the Author

The Counselor's Guide for Facilitating the Interpretation of Dreams: Family and Other Relationship Systems Perspectives (November 2010). New York: Routledge. This book fills practicing counselors and counseling students' great need for training on how to help clients who bring their dreams to counseling, particularly their dreams about relationships. This book is also a resource for earning NBCC-approved continuing education credits at www.yourguidingdreams.com.

Living Dreams, Living Life: A Practical Guide to Understanding Your Dreams and How They Can Change Your Waking Life (2007). Trafford Publishing Company. Also available on Amazon Kindle.

Dreams Guide Professional Writing: Textbook and Writer's Handbook (January 2014). Amazon Kindle.

A Dream-Guided Meditation Model and the Personalized Method for Interpreting Dreams

Evelyn M. Duesbury

Routledge
Taylor & Francis Group
NEW YORK AND LONDON

First published 2017
by Routledge
605 Third Avenue, New York, NY 10017

and by Routledge
2 Park Square, Milton Park, Abingdon, Oxon, OX14 4RN

Routledge is an imprint of the Taylor & Francis Group, an informa business

Library of Congress Cataloging in Publication Data
Names: Duesbury, Evelyn M., 1935-
Title: A dream-guided meditation model and the personalized method for interpreting dreams / Evelyn M. Duesbury.
Description: 1 Edition. | New York : Routledge, 2016. | Includes bibliographical references and index.
Identifiers: LCCN 2016015298| ISBN 9781138693333 (hardback : alk. paper) | ISBN 9781315521657 (ebook)
Subjects: LCSH: Dream interpretation. | Counseling.
Classification: LCC BF1078 .D766 2016 | DDC 154.6/3—dc23
LC record available at https://lccn.loc.gov/2016015298

ISBN: 978-1-138-69333-3 (hbk)
ISBN: 978-1-315-52165-7 (ebk)

Typeset in Times New Roman
by diacriTech, Chennai

This book is dedicated to all dreamers and all meditators—special welcome to newcomers.

Contents

Brief Bio: Evelyn M. Duesbury

Duesbury teaches by writing about use of her researched Personalized Method for Interpreting Dreams (PMID), a thesis-based turn of the twenty-first-century award-winning model. Topics covered in her published works include relationships, counseling, writing, and meditation.

Degrees:
University of Wisconsin-Whitewater: Masters of Counselor Education, 2000
University of Northern Iowa, Cedar Falls, IA: BA in Accounting, May 1978, with Honors,
MBA, May 1984, with Highest Honors

Professional Memberships include:
American Counseling Association (ACA), International Association of Marriage and Family Counselors (IAMFC), Association for Counselor Education and Supervision (ACES), Association of Spiritual, Ethical and Religious Values in Counseling (ASERVIC), Wisconsin Counseling Association (WCA), Illinois Counseling Association (ICA), Illinois Association of Marriage and Family Counselors (IAMFC), Iowa Mental Health Counselors Association (IMHCA), International Association for the Study of Dreams (IASD), and The Honor Society of Phi Kappa Phi, University of Wisconsin–Platteville, WI.

Preface

Several years ago I discovered spirituality teachings that differed from my earlier religious teachings. At the time I was an associate professor of accounting, a career I appreciated so much I had no intention to leave. Then while grading CPA (Certified Public Accounting) exams in New York City, new-to-me spirituality teachings including meditation came to my attention. Nighttime dreams came to my attention and led me to a counselor education masters degree and to the subsequent development of the Dream-Guided Meditation Model.

The dreams that led to the development of the Dream-Guided Meditation Model are herein interpreted with use of the Personalized Method for Interpreting Dreams (PMID). The PMID is a product of my counselor education thesis research, a turn of the twenty-first-century model chosen thesis of the year 2000 by the University of Wisconsin-Whitewater. See Appendix A for the One Hundred Year Turn of the Twenty-First Century Coincidence that resulted in the PMID model.

My aspiration for this book is that it will be a meditation model that is useful in some ways to various people, whatever their gender, race, national origin, religion, or marital status.

Ethics Statement

I agree with this Ethics Statement prepared by the IASD Ethics Committee, 1997 (adapted from www.asdreams.org).

We celebrate the many benefits of dream work, yet we recognize that there are potential risks. We agree with the ethical position taken by the International Association for the Study of Dreams (www.asdreams.org) in that we support an approach to dream work and dream sharing that respects the dreamer's dignity and integrity and that recognizes the dreamer as the decision maker regarding the significance of the dream. Systems of dream work that assign authority or knowledge of the dream's meanings to someone other than the dreamer can be misleading, incorrect, and harmful. Ethical dream work helps the dreamer work with his or her dream images, feelings, and associations and guides the dreamer to experience, appreciate, and understand the dream more fully.

A dreamer's decision to share or discontinue sharing a dream should always be respected and honored. The dreamer should be forewarned that unexpected issues or emotions might arise in the course of the dream work. Information and mutual agreement about the degree of privacy and confidentiality are essential ingredients in creating a safe atmosphere for dream sharing.

Dream work outside a clinical setting is not a substitute for professional counseling or other professional treatment and should not be used as such.

All dreams and interpretations in this book are reprinted with the permission of the dreamer.

Introduction

The immediate goal of the Dream-Guided Meditation Model presented in this book is to attain calmness and peacefulness of body and mind. The ultimate goal from use of the model over time is to become aware of the Higher Self presence within self and all other human beings.

I am one who believes that humans have direct access to Higher Self guidance that is beyond human understanding but is within our experiences. Experiences that convince me are deep meditations and nighttime dreams.

Readers, as you study this book, I expect you may find meditations and nighttime dreams are interactive for you as well. Before you begin your journey though, here's some guiding information about this book's use of the terms meditation and mindfulness, as well as the dream interpretation model used in this book, the Personalized Method for Interpreting Dreams (PMID).

Meditation: Meditation is defined thus: "Emptying the mind of thoughts or concentration of the mind on just one thing" (Encarta® Webster's College Dictionary, 2005). For the purposes of this book, meditation is becoming deeply immersed in quieting the body and slowing the breath, with the prospective goal of becoming aware of your still state.

Mindfulness: Mindful is defined thus: "Fully aware of something" (Encarta® Webster's College Dictionary, 2005). Another definition of mindfulness is: "[T]he practice of maintaining a nonjudgmental state of heightened or complete awareness of one's thoughts, emotions, or experiences on a moment-to-moment basis" (Merriam-Webster Online, 2015). For purposes of this book, mindfulness is maintaining a meditative state as we go about our daily activities.

Research on the use of meditation (and mindfulness) is addressed by several articles on the American Counseling Association website. Go to www.counseling.org and Publications, and then to Counseling Journals. Type "meditation and research" in the question blank, then click on the question symbol. The following is an example from the American Counseling Association website:

> A 4-year qualitative study examined the influence of teaching hatha yoga, meditation, and qigong to counseling graduate students. Participants in the 15-week, 3-credit mindfulness-based stress reduction course reported positive physical, emotional, mental, spiritual, and interpersonal changes and substantial effects on their counseling skills and therapeutic relationships. Students expressed different preferences for and experiences with the 3 mindfulness practices. Most students reported intentions of integrating mindfulness practices into their future profession. (Schure, Christopher, and Christopher, 2008)

Other support for meditation, including research, are as follows.

Miller, Fletcher, and Kabat-Zinn (1995) conducted a follow-up three years after their research on the effects of mindfulness meditation on anxiety disorders:

> A previous study of 22 medical patients with DSM-III-R-defined anxiety disorders showed clinically and statistically significant improvements in subjective and objective symptoms of anxiety and panic following an 8-week outpatient physician-referred group stress reduction intervention based on mindfulness meditation. Twenty subjects demonstrated significant reductions in Hamilton and Beck Anxiety and Depression scores post intervention and at 3-month follow-up. In this study, 3-year follow-up data were obtained and analyzed on 18 of the original 22 subjects to probe long-term effects. Repeated measures analysis showed maintenance of the gains obtained in the original study on the Hamilton [$F(2,32) = 13.22$; $p < 0.001$] and Beck [$F(2,32) = 9.83$; $p < 0.001$] anxiety scales as well as on their respective depression scales, on the Hamilton panic score, the number and severity of panic attacks, and on the Mobility Index-Accompanied and the Fear Survey. A 3-year follow-up comparison of this cohort with a larger group of subjects from the intervention who had met criteria for screening for the original study suggests generalizability of the results obtained with the smaller, more intensively studied cohort. Ongoing compliance with the meditation practice was also demonstrated in the majority of subjects at 3 years. We conclude that an intensive but time-limited group stress reduction intervention based on mindfulness meditation can have long-term beneficial effects in the treatment of people diagnosed with anxiety disorders. (Miller, Fletcher, and Kabat-Zinn, 1995)

According to Cahn and Polich (2006), benefits of meditation include the following:

> Electroencephalographic measures indicate an overall slowing subsequent to meditation, with theta and alpha activation related to proficiency of practice. Sensory evoked potential assessment of concentrative meditation yields amplitude and latency changes for some components and practices. Cognitive event-related potential evaluation of meditation implies that practice changes attentional allocation. Neuroimaging studies indicate increased regional cerebral blood flow measures during meditation. Taken together, meditation appears to reflect changes in anterior cingulate cortex and dorsolateral prefrontal areas. Neurophysiological meditative state and trait effects are variable but are beginning to demonstrate consistent outcomes for research and clinical applications.

According to Barret et al. (2012), meditation or exercise may reduce ARI (acute respiratory infection):

> Compared with control, global severity was significantly lower for meditation (P = .004). Both global severity and total days of illness (duration) trended toward being lower for the exercise group (P=.16 and P=.032, respectively), as did illness duration for the meditation group (P=.034).

A nighttime dream brought the meditation model presented in this book. However, readers can learn the meditation model without learning how to interpret their dreams. For those who want to explore use of the dream interpretation model I use in this book, this next section includes the full Personalized Method for Interpreting Dreams (PMID) model plus research and guidance on using the model.

First a caution: For those who have negative and fearful dreams, read Appendix B, Caveat on Bad and Worrisome Dreams by Edward Bruce Bynum, before you attempt to work alone with your dreams.

Personalized Method for Interpreting Dreams (PMID)

With the PMID model the dreamer interprets his or her dreams. When a counselor is involved, the dreamer is still the interpreter; the counselor facilitates the process. With or without counselor facilitation, learning to use the PMID model takes time. During our research and exploration projects the average time for participants to successfully use the model was eight weeks, and that was when one researcher facilitated participants' use of the model.

So now we begin presentation of the model. First are the formal PMID model steps followed by the Purposes of Each PMID Model step, Suggestions for Dream Recall and Recording, and then Research and Explorations of the PMID Model. To increase your confidence in the model, note that it is an award-winning model and by coincidence was published at the turn of the twenty-first century (see Appendix A for the One Hundred Year Turn of the Twenty-First Century Coincidence that resulted in the PMID model).

Formal Personalized Method for Interpreting Dreams (PMID)

PMID Step 1: Connect your previous day (often the day before) event(s) to the dream to discover the theme of this dream. The events may appear in either symbolic or literal terms in your dream. Write down the appropriate events and record when they occurred.

PMID Step 2: Connect your previous day (often the day before) thoughts to your dream to detect which thoughts may have prompted this dream's responses and provide thought-questions that this dream responds to. Similar to events, your thoughts may appear in your dream in either symbolic or literal terms. Write "I thought" statements and record when you thought them.

PMID Step 3: Select and define major words and phrases from your write-up of this dream to discover the personalized meanings of the dream. Consider effects of day-before-your-dream events, thoughts, and earlier experiences on the meaning of each major dream phrase and symbol. The general definition for phrases as used in this step is "a string of words," which can be phrases, clauses, or whole sentences.

PMID Step 4: Compare your emotions in your dream with your pre-dream, waking-life emotions to discover whether your waking-life emotions accurately reflect how you feel about the issue in this dream. Note that the issue may be a relationship issue. What differences, if any, do you find between your emotions in your dream and your waking-life emotions? It is useful to periodically review your emotions in your dreams about the main issue or relationship.

PMID Step 5: Explore your dream for possible solutions to problems or for changing (or affirming) your thoughts, attitudes, or behaviors. Consider your responses to each PMID model step, including Step 6, as you search for solutions and suggestions in this dream. Give primary attention to the power of your before-your-dream thoughts (PMID Step 2) to act as questions that your dream answers.

PMID Step 6: Explore your dream for family and other relationship systems perspectives (influences arising from reactions to family and other major relationships, past and current) to discover whether this dream reflects your reactions during earlier experiences with your family or other major relationships. Compare and comment on your dreaming and your waking-life reactions to the primary relationships in this dream.

A book for counselors to study the PMID model is *The Counselor's Guide for Facilitating the Interpretation of Dreams: Families and Other Relationship Systems Perspectives* (Routledge).

A book for the general public to study the PMID model is *Living Dreams, Living Life: A Practical Guide to Understanding Your Dreams and How They Can Change Your Waking Life* (Trafford and Amazon Kindle).

A book for writers to study is *Dreams Guide Professional Writing: Textbook and Writer's Handbook* (Amazon Kindle).

Purposes of Each PMID Model Step (Adapted from Duesbury, 2010, pp. 37–38)

"The purpose of Step 1 (connect your day-before-your-dream events to this dream) is to uncover the theme of the dream."

> The purpose of Step 2 (connect day-before-your-dream thoughts to this dream) is to determine whether the dream responds to any of the dreamer's pre-dream (often day-before-the-dream) thoughts. Our thoughts . . . frequently act as questions the dream answers.

Dream researchers have long recognized that thoughts passing through the waking mind are frequent and significant initiators of dreams (Kramer, Roth, Arand, and Bonnet, 1981, pp. 83–86).

"The purpose of Step 3 (select and define major words and phrases from your write-up of this dream) is to find personal meanings for phrases (strings of words) taken directly from our recalled dream."

"The purpose of Step 4 (compare your emotions in your dream with your pre-dream waking-life emotions about the issue in this dream) is to discover whether our dreaming emotions" differ from our waking life appraisal of those emotions. Dreaming emotions, though often exaggerated, are often more accurate than our waking-life appraisal.

> The purpose of Step 5 (explore your dream for possible solutions to problems, including changing [or affirming] thoughts, attitudes, or behaviors) is to assimilate all the responses from the other steps (including Step 6) to arrive at solutions to problems or issues the dreamer

is facing. Solutions and suggestions are often connected to the waking life events and thoughts that prompted this dream.
The purpose of Step 6 (explore your dream for family and relationship systems perspectives) is for the dreamer to determine whether the dream contains information about his or her reactions (past or current) during relationship experiences, and if so, how those reactions affect his or her current functioning.

I used the PMID model for all dreams in this book. However, it was May 2000 before I had completely developed the PMID steps for my Counselor Education master thesis. Consequently, for many earlier dreams I was unaware of the importance of recording pre-dream events (PMID Step 1), pre-dream thoughts (PMID Step 2), and pre-dream emotions (PMID Step 4). Thus, this critical information is missing for some dreams in this book.

Though I used the PMID model for all dreams in this book, I show alternatively formal steps, brief form steps, and blending the action of the steps with my narrative interpretations. That practice came from a dream in which one of my professors, one I have great respect for, advised me to blend the action of the steps with my narrative interpretations.

Suggestions for Dream Recall and Recording (Excerpts from Duesbury, 2007, pp. 12–13)

Dream Recall

When you wake, lie very still, remain in a relaxed, almost drowsy state, and wait for dream recall to emerge into your mind.

Keep a pad and pencil near your bed, or keep a tape recorder near your bed and write the dream down (or voice record it if you prefer) as soon as you wake.

Be alert for dream recall during the day, especially during relaxed times.

How to Record Your Dream

Record your dreams in the first person and present tense to foster the immediate and intimate feelings of the dream. Include your dreaming emotions in the dream narrative itself, since emotions are integral parts of the dreaming experience. Record every recalled detail of the dream, regardless of its seeming relatedness or importance. Often seeming insignificant details are keys to developing dream meanings later.

Retain the dream script as originally written. Dreams contain suggestions for improving the dreamer's circumstances. If we change the dream to fit our derived meanings, we might distort the dream's helpful suggestions.

Research and Explorations of the PMID Model

The PMID model is a product of Duesbury's year 2000 thesis. Subsequent to the thesis Duesbury and colleagues refined the model during three more research projects and four explorations (Internal Review not requested). Results of those projects are shown in Duesbury (2010, pp. 199–216). Abbreviated results are next.

Duesbury and colleagues developed three instruments to research and explore participants' use of the PMID model. Those instruments are:

- A Screening Instrument to appraise applicants' emotional ability to work with their dreams
- A Periodic Feedback Instrument (PFI) for participants to rate their abilities to do each PMID model step
- An Emotional Change Instrument (ECI) for participants to increase self-awareness of their emotions regarding the people about whom they dream

Researchers compared participants' PFI and ECI ratings with participants' dreams and PMID interpretations. Some brief results follow.

Periodic Feedback Instrument (PFI) Results (first used with Project 3)

Project 3 (4-month exploration, 81 dreams, 11 participants): Average time for participants to learn the PMID model during facilitation by a facilitator was eight weeks.

Emotional Change Instruments (ECI) Results (first used with Project 3)

Project 3 (4-month exploration, 81 dreams): At 14 weeks all 11 participants' ECIs showed positive changes in dreaming emotions about one or more relationships.

Project 4 (4-months exploration, 36 dreams): At 14 weeks four of the five participants' ECIs showed positive changes in dreaming emotions about one or more relationships.

Project 5 (4-month exploration, 29 dreams): At 14 weeks four of the six participants' ECIs showed positive changes in dreaming emotions about one or more relationships.

Project 6 (6 months of research, 200 dreams): At 6 months five of the seven (an injury curtailed one participant's final reporting) participants' ECIs showed positive changes in dreaming emotions about one or more relationships. Participants' ECIs showed emotions in dreams differed from waking-life emotions for 46 dreams, with 43 more positive in dreams than in waking-life appraisal of emotions. The co-investigator's examinations of all ECIs agreed with all but one ECI rating by one participant.

Research Support for Use of Each PMID Model Step (As presented in Duesbury, 2010, pp. 62, 69, 78, 87, 93, 102)

Duesbury and colleagues conducted seven projects. All seven projects showed success with using the PMID model steps. For brevity, the results of one project, the last (Project 6), is presented here: Okocha and Duesbury (2005–2006), 6 months of research, 8 participants until the final report (an injury curtained one participant's final report), 200 dreams. Wilcoxon signed-rank tests–critical values of W for samples less than 10 (http://vassarstats.net/textbook/ch12a.html) was used to rate results.

PMID Step 1: Previous-day event connections: Significant at 2 1/2 months: W = 33 ns/r = 8, $p \leq .05$, at 6 months: Nonsignificant
PMID Step 2: Previous-day thought connections: Significant at 2 1/2 months: W = 34 ns/r = 8, $p \leq .02$, at 6 months: W = 21 ns/r = 6, p ≤ .05
PMID Step 3, Dream phrases defined: At 2 1/2 months: W = 30 ns/r = 8, $p \leq .05$, At 6 months: W = 28 ns/r = 7, $p \leq .02$
PMID Step 4: Dreaming emotions compared with pre-dream emotions: At 2 1/2 months: W = 28 ns/r = 7, $p \leq .02$, at 6 months: Nonsignificant
PMID Step 5: Find solutions: At 2 1/2 months: W = 26 ns/r = 7, p ≤ .05, at 6 months: Nonsignificant
PMID Step 6: Systems perspectives present in dreams: At 2 1/2 months: W = 28 ns/r = 7, $p \leq .02$, at 6 months: W = 21 ns/r = 6, $p \leq .05$

Dream Specialists' Support for Elements in the PMID Model

Pre-Dream Events (PMID Step 1)

Freud (1900/1955) connected previous-day events to the dream as one step of interpreting the dream.

Domhoff (2003) conducted studies of eight people's dream diaries and concluded dreams connect to dreamers' waking-life interests.

Strauch and Meier's (1996) research found that participants' dreams connected to previous day events.

Cartwright and Lamberg's (2000) sleep laboratory studies found pre-dream events are present in dreams, though some of the events occurred a week or so earlier.

Hartmann (1968) found a high percentage of events and thoughts incorporated in his study of 800 of his own dreams.

Pre-Dream Thoughts (PMID Step 2)

Freud (1900/1955) claimed "Dreams show a clear preference for the impressions of the immediately preceding days" (p. 163).

Kramer, Roth, Arand, and Bonnet (1981) wrote that researchers have long supported pre-dream thoughts as initiators of dreams.

Schredl (2006) declared that pre-dream thought connections to dreams show the continuity between waking and dreaming.

Dreamer's Experiences Help the Dreamer Interpret the Dream (PMID Step 3)

Synesius of Cyrene (cited in Kelsey, 1991) wrote that dreamers are the best ones to interpret their dreams because dreams are "within us" (p. 251, par. 3).

Hildebrant (1895, cited in Van de Castle, 1994) contended every image in the dream can be defined, given sufficient time.

Delaney (1988, 1996) supported that dream images come from the dreamer's experiences.

LaBerge (2004) agreed the source of dreams is the dreamer's experiences.

Emotions in Dreams (PMID Step 4)

Hartmann (2001, 1998) wrote, "dreams make connections more widely, more broadly, than waking and . . . the connections are guided by emotion" (p. 11). Cartwright and Lamberg (2000) learned from their studies that though people denied stressful emotions during waking life, they readily recognized those emotions in their dreams.

Jung (1966) supported that emotions in dreams connect to the dreamer's waking life; thus work with dreams leads to stress reduction.

Dreams Contain Answers to Waking Life Thought-Questions (PMID Step 5)

Cartwright and Lamberg (2000) wrote that dreams can tell us about issues that need to be addressed before we are aware of those issues during our waking states.

Krippner and Dilliard (1988) wrote: "We believe your nighttime adventures can teach you methods of creative problem-solving that may dramatically improve your personal and professional life" (p. 1).

Siegel (2002) also wrote that dreams reveal answers to our waking-life needs.

Synesius of Cyrene (cited in Kelsey 1991) wrote: "Many of the things which present difficulties to us awake, some of these it makes completely clear while we are asleep, and others it helps us explain" (p. 248, par. 9).

Delaney wrote in several of her books, one from 1993, that our dreams respond to questions within our waking-life thoughts and bring answers to those thoughts.

Family and Other Relationship Systems Perspectives in Dreams (PMID Step 6)

Cartwright and Lamberg (2000) wrote: "[D]reams review the experiences that give rise to strong feelings and match them to related images from the past" (p. 269).

Hartmann (1995) wrote that dreams "often seem to be dealing with interpersonal problems, with the dreamer's current concerns about family, friends, lovers" (pp. 213–228).

Krippner and Dillard (1988) wrote that the images in the memory bank of our minds "sometimes go all the way back to childhood, and are in some way related to the current issue" (p. 52).

Now let us learn how nighttime dreams and meditations (inner work) flow together. That's how it is for me. The dream *Dream Work and Inner Work Flow Together* shown next answered my previous day's thought-question: "Could my dreams replace my meditations?"

Meditations and Dreams

DREAM: DREAM WORK AND INNER WORK FLOW TOGETHER

There are two drain spouts running along two roofs. I look and see where the spouts almost come together in the middle. One somehow dumps into the other drain spout.

Words in my mind when I woke were: "This dream work and inner work are for me."

> **PMID Step 1:** Connect your previous day (often the day before) events to the dream to discover the theme of this dream.

Last night I read a writer-meditator's account on how he knows he must meditate.

PMID Step 2: Connect your previous day (often the day before) thoughts to your dream to detect which thoughts may have prompted this dream's responses. Write "I thought" statements and record when you thought them.

Last night, after I read the writer-meditator's account on how he knows he must meditate, I thought about my meditations and how at times when my meditation success is low, I wonder if my dreams could replace meditations. So, a possible thought-question is: "Could my dreams replace my meditations?"

PMID Step 3: Select and define major words and phrases from your write-up of this dream to discover the dream's personalized meanings. The general definition for "phrases" as used in this step is "a string of words," which can be phrases, clauses, or whole sentences.

- **Two drain spouts running along two roofs:** The thoughts in my mind as I woke ("This dream work and inner work are for me.") identify the two drain spouts as dreams (dream work) and meditations (inner work).
- **Look and see where the spouts almost come together in the middle:** Dreams and meditations almost come together.
- **One somehow dumps into the other drain spout:** Meditations and dreams appear in succession instead of one replacing the other.

The response to my pre-dreams thought-question of whether my dreams could replace my meditations is: "Dreams and meditations are interactive with each other; both are resourceful."

Now I repeat: "Readers, as you study this book you may find nighttime dreams and meditations are interactive for you."

Synopsis of This Book

Sections A and B present detailed coverage of the Dream-Guided Meditation Model. In Section A, Chapter 1 presents the dream that brought the meditation model. Chapters 2, 3, and 4 present stages of the model as clarified and detailed by dreams subsequent to the dream that brought the model. Chapter 5 presents prospective results from use of the Dream-Guided Meditation Model over time. In Section B, Chapters 6 and 7 present dreams about when and where to meditate. A conclusion and a summary of lessons presented in this book finish *A Dream-Guided Meditation Model and the Personalized Method for Interpreting Dreams*.

References

Barrett, B., Hayney, M. S., Muller, D., Rakel, D., Ward, A., Obasi, C. N., . . . Coe, C. L. (2012). Meditation or exercise for preventing acute respiratory infection: A randomized controlled trial. *Annals of Family Medicine*, Jul-Aug; *10*(4), 337–346. doi: 10.1370/afm.1376.

Cahn, B. R., & Polich, J. (March 2006). Meditation states and traits: EEG, ERP, and neuroimaging studies. *Psychological Bulletin*, *132*(2), 180–211. doi:10.1037/0033-2909.132.2.180. PMID 16536641.

Cartwright R., & Lamberg, L. (1992). *Crisis dreaming: Using your dreams to solve your problems*. New York: HarperCollins (Lincoln, NE: ASJA Press, 2000).

Delaney, G. (1988, 1996). *Living your dreams*. New York: HarperCollins.

Domhoff, G. W. (2003). *The scientific study of dreams: Neural networks, cognitive development, and content analysis*. Washington, D. C.: American Psychological Association.

Duesbury, E. M. (2007). *Living dreams, living life: A practical guide to understanding your dreams and how they can change your waking life*. Canada: Trafford and Amazon Kindle.

Duesbury, E. M. (2010). *The counselor's guide for facilitating the interpretation of dreams: Family and other relationship systems perspectives*. New York: Routledge.

Encarta® Webster's College Dictionary (2nd ed.). (2005). New York: Bloomsbury.

Freud, S. (1955). *The interpretation of dreams* (J. Strachey, Trans. and Ed.). New York: Basic Books (original work published 1900).

Hartmann, E. (1968). The day residue: Time distribution of waking events. *Psychophysiology*, *5*(2), 222.

Hartmann, E. (1995). Making connections in a safe place: Is dreaming psychotherapy? *Dreaming, Journal of the Association for the Study of Dreams*, *5*(4), 213–228.

Hartmann, E. (1998, 2001). *Dreams and nightmares: The origin and meaning of dreams*. Cambridge, MA: Perseus.

Jung, C. G. (1966). *Two essays on analytical psychology* (R. F. C. Hull, Trans.). Princeton, NJ: Bollingen Series/Princeton University Press.

Kramer, M., Roth, T., Arand, D., & Bonnet, M. (1981). Waking and dreaming mentation: A test of their interrelationship. *Neuroscience Letters*, *22*, 83–86.

Krippner, S., & Dillard, J. (1988). *Dreamworking: How to use your dreams for creative problem-solving*. New York: Bearly, Limited.

LaBerge, S. (2004). *Lucid dreaming*. Boulder, CO: Sounds True.

Miller, J. J., Fletcher, K., & Kabat-Zinn, J. (May 1995). Three-year follow-up and clinical implications of a mindfulness meditation-based stress reduction intervention in the treatment of anxiety disorders. *General Hospital Psychiatry*, *17*(3), 192–200. Department of Psychiatry, University of Massachusetts Medical Center, Worcester 01655, USA. Retrieved February 2, 2016, from http://sv.mediyoga.com/publication/download/three-year-follow-up-and-clinical-implications-of-a-mindfulness-meditation-based-stress-reduction-intervention-in-the-treatment-of-anxiety-disorders-miller-jj-fletcher-k-kabat-zinn-j/.

Mindfulness. (n.d.). In *Merriam-Webster Online*. Retrieved February 13, 2015 from www.merriam-webster.com/dictionary/mindfulness.

Schure, M. B., Christopher, J., & Christopher, S. (2008). Mind–body medicine and the art of self-care: Teaching mindfulness to counseling students through yoga, meditation, and qigong. *Journal of Counseling & Development*, *86*(1), 47–56. doi: 10.1002/j.1556-6678.2008.tb00625.x.

Schredl, M. (2006). Factors affecting the continuity between waking and dreaming: Emotional intensity and emotional tone of the waking-life event. *Sleep and Hypnosis*, *8*(1), 1–5.
Siegel. A. (2002). *Dream wisdom: Uncovering life's answers in your dreams*. Berkley/Toronto: Celestial Arts.
Strauch, I., & Meier, B. (1996). *In search of dreams: Results of experimental dream research*. Albany: State University of New York Press.
Synesius of Cyrene. *On dreams* (excerpts cited in M. T. Kelsey, *God, dreams, and revelation*. Minneapolis, MN: Augsburg Books, 1991, p. 251).
Van de Castle, R. L. (1994). *Our dreaming mind*. New York: Ballantine, a Division of Random House.

Section A

The Meditation Model

1 The Dream That Brought the Dream-Guided Meditation Model

What a captivating feature for the inner counselor, the dreaming mind, to answer people's waking-life thought-questions. Thought-questions are waking-life thoughts with the potential to prompt nighttime dreams that contain responsive solutions or answers. Such is the case with most dreams in this book. Read this first chapter to discover what thoughts or thought-questions brought the meditation model that is the reason this book came into being. Then absorb yourself in discovery of the basic steps of the meditation model.

DREAM: A MEDITATION MODEL GIVEN IN A DREAM

Mr. Sampson (pseudonym—to protect confidentiality) *walks with me to the gymnasium at the school I attended during grade and high school. Mr. Sampson says something about a college and I think he is talking about something for himself, but he continues, "But then who would teach your classes?" I realize he is telling me about a college for me, and I exclaim, "Oh, Mr. Sampson, you found a college for me!" I start to tell him I have been wavering about going to a college, but now I make a decision, "But, yes, I'll go. Where is it?"*

He says two words that I come to understand as "body quieter." Then he says, "Arizona State," words that are clear to me. At the end he says one word that is also clear to me . . . a word I realize symbolizes the Higher Self potential present in all persons. I say, "Oh, Mr. Samson, I think that would be good."

As I wake, the words I heard in my dream are being spoken in my ears, almost like a voice buzzing beside my ears; the sensation is so real. So I hear the last words in my dream as well as in my physical ears as I wake.

PMID Step 1: Connect your previous day (often the day before) events to the dream to discover the theme of this dream.

Before this dream I searched a bit for a college to prepare me for some kind of spirituality work. A possible theme of this dream is: Spirituality work.

PMID Step 2: Connect your previous day (often the day before) thoughts to your dream to detect which thoughts may have prompted this dream's responses. Write "I thought" statements and record when you thought them.

Before this dream I wavered in my thoughts on whether to enroll in such a college, the college I later realized is a meditation model. A possible thought-question this dream responds to is: "Should I go to a college to prepare for some kind of spirituality work?"

PMID Step 3: Select and define major words and phrases from your write-up of this dream to discover the dream's personalized meanings. The general definition for "phrases" as used in this step is "a string of words," which can be phrases, clauses, or whole sentences.

- **Walks with me to the gymnasium at the school I attended during grade and high school:** A major transition in my life occurred when the high school basketball coach chose an eighth-grader (me) to be on first team. Here, I believe the gymnasium represents a transition that will make a major change in my life.
- **Body quieter:** Quiet Your Body fits well as a first step of meditation.
- **Arizona State:** Words that are clear to me during the dream. Arizona State translates into "air zone state."
- **"Ar":** Represents "air" or breath.
- **"Zone":** Represents a zone within where one can find a still state.
- **Word I realize symbolizes the Higher Self potential present in all persons:** The word I heard applies to my spirituality beliefs. It is a word that, as this phrase shows, "symbolizes the Higher Self potential present in all persons," not only to my spirituality beliefs.

PMID Step 4: Compare your emotions in your dream with your pre-dream, waking-life emotions to discover whether your waking-life emotions accurately reflect how you feel about the issue in this dream. Note that the issue may be a relationship issue. What differences, if any, do you find between your emotions in your dream and your waking-life emotions? It is useful to periodically review your emotions in your dreams regarding the main issue or relationship at hand.

In my dream I am exuberant about the school Mr. Samson found for me. In the waking state, before this dream, I felt anxiety to find a school. Note: Researchers claim that emotions in dreams, though often exaggerated, are most often more accurate than the person's waking-life appraisal of emotions about the issue in the dream. (Hartmann [2001,

p. 11] claims "dreams make connections more widely, more broadly, than waking and . . . the connections are guided by emotion.")

PMID Step 5: Explore your dream for possible solutions to problems, including changing (or affirming) your thoughts, attitudes, or behaviors. Consider your responses to each PMID model step, including Step 6, as you search for solutions and suggestions in this dream. Give primary attention to the power of your thoughts before your dream (PMID Step 2) to act as questions that your dream answers.

My dream shows how to meditate. These words tell me to go to the school within myself. I sincerely believe the words I heard spoken within my dream and heard as a voice buzzing beside my ears as I woke were steps for a meditation model. I believe that model may be useful for people from various religions. I say that from having taken a course at a school of religion on World Religions. The textbook for that course was Houston Smith's 1991 book *The World's Religions*. The world religions presented in Smith's book are Hinduism, Buddhism, Confucianism, Taoism, Islam, Judaism, and Christianity. These religions might have figures that would relate to the interpretations I found for this dream.

PMID Step 6: Explore your dream for family and other relationships shown or implicated in the dream to discover whether this dream reflects your reactions during earlier experiences with your family or other major relationships.

The major relationship in this dream is Mr. Sampson. I'll explain a bit about him so you understand why I value his suggestions. He is an official at the university where I am teaching at the time of this dream. A prominent characteristic I associate with Mr. Sampson is his encouragement for innovative projects. My reactions to his waking-life encouragements support the college he tells me about in this dream. However, I discovered the college is really a meditation model, the Dream-Guided Meditation Model presented in this book.

My PMID Step 3 definitions reveal three stages in the Dream-Guided Meditation Model:

- Stage One: Quiet Your Whole Body (See Chapter 2 for an expanded explanation of the Quiet Your Whole Body stage.)
- Stage Two: Slow Your Breath (See Chapter 3 for an expanded explanation of the Slow Your Breath stage.)
- Stage Three: Still Your Thoughts and Listen to Become Aware of Your Still State (See Chapter 4 for an expanded explanation of the Still Your Thoughts and Listen to Become Aware of Your Still State stage.)

In Chapter 5, we expand upon the potential benefit of using the Dream-Guided Meditation Model, that is, becoming conscious of your Higher Self, a presence in all human beings that is latent until discovered within your being.

Readers, to gain confidence in the above PMID Step 3 interpretations, notice all the dreams that support these interpretations as you read this book.

Summary of Chapter 1

This chapter presents the dream that inspired the Dream-Guided Meditation Model. From this dream I have interpreted a three-stage process that will yield meditative results from quieting your whole body, slowing your breath, and stilling your thoughts and listening to become aware of your still state. The dream includes a word that symbolizes the Higher Self potential present in all persons, which is latent until discovered: this is the ultimate goal of the Dream-Guided Meditation Model.

References

Hartmann, E. (1998, 2001). *Dreams and nightmares: The origin and meaning of dreams*. Cambridge, MA: Perseus.

Smith, H. (1991). *The world's religions*. New York: HarperOne.

2 Stage One—Quiet Your Whole Body

As Chapter 1 shows, I interpreted the words "body quieter" from the Dream-Guided Meditation Model as the Quiet Your Body stage. Quiet Your Body is a common first stage of meditation. How many of you who have some knowledge of meditation or who meditate yourself and/or counsel clients about meditation procedures know that a standard first stage in meditation is Quiet Your Body?

So what portion of your body do you quiet? The upper portion, the lower portion, or the whole body? Notice, the meditation model dream didn't include that detail. However, the next dream does include the detail for how much of the body to quiet.

DREAM: USE THE FULL TREE FOR MEDITATION

There are trees—seems to be three. The tree I notice is a medium-sized tree. I particularly notice that tree has no trunk.

PMID Step 1: Connect your previous day (often the day before) events to the dream to discover the theme of this dream.

The night before this dream, I began to use the first part of a meditation model that is different from the Dream-Guided Meditation Model. The part of the other meditation model I used was "relax half the body." When I relaxed the top half of my body, tightness developed in my left chest, not relaxation.

PMID Step 2: Connect your previous day (often the day before) thoughts to your dream to detect which thoughts may have prompted this dream's responses. Write "I thought" statements and record when you thought them.

Last night when the tightness came in my chest during my use of the other meditation model, I wondered if the tightness came from only relaxing half my body. So, an obvious thought-question this dream responds to is: "Did the tightness come from only relaxing half my body?"

PMID Step 3: Select and define major words and phrases from your write-up of this dream to discover the dream's personalized meanings. The general definition for "phrases" as used in this step is "a string of words," which can be phrases, clauses, or whole sentences.

- **Trees:** In the context of having a relaxed body for meditation, trees could symbolize human bodies. A dream dictionary universal meaning of tree is "support (trunk) . . ." (Boushahla and Reidel-Geubtner, 1992, p. 108).
- **Tree I notice is a medium-sized tree:** In the context of this dream, the new-to-me meditation model I used last night is a model that relaxes half the body.
- **Particularly notice the tree has no trunk:** This is symbolic of quieting only the upper half of my body for meditation. This method has no trunk, no support, in the bottom half of the body.

The dream responds to my pre-dream thought-question about whether the tightness came from drawing the breath through only half the body. The dream reveals it's best for my Dream-Guided Meditation Model to quiet the whole body.

How to Use This Dream: For Stage One of the Dream-Guided Meditation Model, quiet the whole body. A suggestion for quieting the body is to first quiet the part of your body where you most feel tension. Then let a relaxed feeling ripple downward in waves from your medulla oblongata, the continuation of the spinal cord within the skull that forms the lowest part of the brainstem and contains control centers for the heart and lungs, to the bottom of your feet and then back through your body. Continue this relaxation until your whole body is quieted.

And quiet means extreme quiet. A person whose teachings led me to meditation came in a dream and demonstrated the quietness needed for deep meditation. That dream is a response to my pre-dream thoughts on whether, when I wake and am restless during the night, should I, like Edison, who professed to sleep only four hours at a time, get up when I wake and work? Here's the answering dream and the teaching.

DREAM: THE TEACHER SITS IN EXTREME QUIET FOR MEDITATION

I am sitting beside the teacher on a bench in my parents' kitchen. . . . This is where we live, though, here in my parents' house. I don't think it strange. . . . However, it is only the kitchen that resembles my parents' house.

This is during the night and the teacher's wife is in bed in the guest bedroom.

As I sit here beside the teacher he is so quiet I wonder if he has died. I realize later [in the dream] *he is alive. He just sits so very quiet it had seemed he could have passed on. I feel honored he is here.*

PMID Step 1: Connect your previous day (often the day before) events to the dream to discover the theme of this dream.

Before this dream was one of the nights when I woke and was restless. Then I went back to sleep and dreamed this dream.

Yesterday I prepared a "Thinking of You" card for the wife of the teacher in this dream as the teacher passed away shortly before I had this dream.

PMID Step 2: Connect your previous day (often the day before) thoughts to your dream to detect which thoughts may have prompted this dream's responses. Write "I thought" statements and record when you thought them.

Before this dream I wondered whether, when I wake and am restless during the night, should I, like Edison, who professed to sleep only four hours at a time, get up when I wake and work.

PMID Step 3: Select and define major words and phrases from your write-up of this dream to discover the dream's personalized meanings. The general definition for "phrases" as used in this step is "a string of words," which can be phrases, clauses, or whole sentences.

- **This is where we live, though, here in my parent's house:** This is where I grew up and where I first learned religious teachings. I never heard of meditation until, on a business trip in adult life, I happened to attend the teacher's spirituality center.
- **Only the kitchen resembles my parents' house:** The kitchen was my mother's domain, and she was the parent who took my siblings and me to church.
- **During the night:** Responds to my pre-dream thoughts on whether when I wake and am restless during the night I should get up and work when I have difficulty going back to sleep.
- **Teacher's wife is in bed in the guest bedroom:** This ties to my previous day's thoughts about her as I prepared a "Thinking of You" card for her. Her husband, the teacher, had passed away shortly before this dream.
- **So quiet I wonder if he has died:** Though later in the dream *I realize he is alive*, the teacher had passed on from this life. He is alive in this dream to teach how quiet the body needs to be for meditation.

The answer to my last night's thoughts on whether, when I wake during the night, I should get up and work is: "When you wake during the night and feel restless, meditate, but meditate in extreme quiet."

Summary of Chapter 2

This chapter expands the Quiet the Body stage of the Dream-Guided Meditation Model to Quiet the Whole Body. That change comes from the dream *Use the Full Tree for Meditation*. Another dream, *The Teacher Sits in Extreme Quiet for Meditation*, shows it is necessary to become extremely quiet during meditation.

Reference

Boushahla, J. & Reidel-Geubtner, V. (1992). *The dream dictionary*. New York: Berkley.

3 Stage Two—Slow Your Breath

As shown in Chapter 1 and the dream that brought the Dream-Guided Meditation Model, the words "Arizona State" were clear during the dream and as I woke. No guessing: The words were "Arizona State." To interpret Arizona State, I simply broke the word "Arizona" into parts. The first part is interpreted thus:

Ar = Air = breath. Attention to the breath is often a major part of meditation.

Yet, a detail the meditation model dream didn't explain was what kind of breaths to take. This chapter does explain what kind of breaths to take.

So now we begin with the breath stage. One night after wondering whether to take even or uneven breaths, I had an answering dream.

DREAM: PLAY THE METRONOME SLOWLY AND UNEVEN BEATS ARE OKAY

I am playing a metronome. A teacher tells me to slow the beats. While the teacher is here in the dream, I ask her whether the time between beats needs to be even or whether uneven time between the beats is okay. The teacher says, "It doesn't matter whether the beats are even or uneven."

PMID Step 1: Connect your previous day (often the day before) events to the dream to discover the theme of this dream.

The night before this dream I continued to read instructions for a meditation model that is different from the Dream-Guided Meditation Model. I was expecting more instructions to come in the mail.

PMID Step 2: Connect your previous day (often the day before) thoughts to your dream to detect which thoughts may have prompted this dream's responses. Write "I thought" statements and record when you thought them.

The night before this dream I wondered whether to take even or uneven breaths during Stage Two of the Dream-Guided Meditation Model.

PMID Step 3: Select and define major words and phrases from your write-up of this dream to discover the dream's personalized meanings. The general definition for "phrases" as used in this step is "a string of words," which can be phrases, clauses, or whole sentences.

- **Playing the metronome:** "Patented in 1815 by Johann Maelzel, the metronome is an instrument used to keep time for music" (Metronome, n.d.). Keeping time for music in this dream symbolizes breaths during meditation.
- **Teacher tells me to slow the beats:** Guidance on how to breathe during meditation—take slower breaths.
- **While the teacher is here in the dream:** This likely comes from thinking about the instructions I expect to come in the mail for the new-to-me meditation model.
- **Ask her whether the time between beats needs to be even or whether uneven time between the beats is okay:** This is a questioning thought I had the night before this dream.
- **"Doesn't matter whether the beats are even or uneven":** Answer to my pre-dream questioning thought. The beats, the breaths, can be unevenly spaced.

PMID Step 5: Explore your dream for possible solutions to problems, including changing (or affirming) your thoughts, attitudes, or behaviors.

I am given the answers needed about what kind of breaths to take: Slow the breath, and it doesn't matter whether the breaths are even or unevenly spaced.

How I've Used This Dream: I continue to use the fine suggestions the teacher gave to me in this dream: Slow the breaths, and there is no need to take evenly spaced breaths. Later, I had dream advice to abandon the meditation model I had been investigating when I had the dream I am discussing here. I am grateful, though, to have studied it long enough for these fine suggestions on the kind of breaths to take.

Vital Tip

Before we go on, here's a vital tip. Notice and remember as you meditate and when you help others with the meditation model, especially beginner meditators: Benefits accrue from these first two meditation stages without going further: Quiet Your Whole Body (sit in extreme quiet), and

Slow Your Breath (uneven breaths are okay). These meditation stages relax the meditator for the day ahead. One of my first spirituality teachers said, "Nothing may happen." Yet relaxation most always occurs, which is truly well worth the time spent. Focus within your being and let relaxation occur.

Use these two stages before you start work each day, perhaps for ten-minute meditations. The more you practice, the better the results that usually occur.

Summary of Chapter 3

This chapter expands the breath stage of the Dream-Guided Meditation Model. The breath stage is from the first part of the word "Arizona": Ar = Air = breath. A dream, *Play the Metronome Slowly and Uneven Beats Are Okay*, clarified the kind of breaths to take. A vital tip is given: Benefits accrue from these first two meditation stages (Quiet Your Whole Body and Slow Your Breath). These two stages relax the meditator for the day ahead without going further.

For those who choose to go further with the Dream-Guided Meditation Model, the next chapter describes Stage Three of the meditation: Still Your Thoughts and Listen to Become Aware of Your Still State.

Reference

Metronome. (n.d.). In *How stuff works*. Retrieved January 14, 2014 from http://electronics.howstuffworks.com/gadgets/audio-music/metronome.htm.

4 Stage Three—Still Your Thoughts and Listen to Become Aware of Your Still State

Readers, we now extend the meaning of the words "Arizona State," which came in the Dream-Guided Meditation Model dream presented in Chapter 1. Stage three of the model originates from the words "Arizona State." Here's how: The second part of the phrase "Arizona State" is "zona state." Zona state is translated as the still state.

Yet the meditation model dream didn't show how to become aware of the still state. The dreams elucidated in this chapter do show how to become aware of the still state, which is not as easy as it may seem; the dreams in this chapter will illustrate that fact.

Thoughts are a major interference with becoming aware of the still state. Thoughts, meandering thoughts, and even directed thoughts can interfere with the ability to become aware of the still state. The first dreams in this chapter show how to still the thoughts. Then the next dreams address listening. The last dreams in this chapter center on becoming aware of the still state, which is the ultimate goal of Stage Three.

Possible responses from becoming aware of the still state include intuitive knowing, peacefulness, and even at times feelings of love. Whether intuitive knowing or peacefulness or feelings of love occur during or after your meditations, be grateful for whatever success you gain. Relaxation most always occurs. Feeling discouraged (as I have at times) interferes with success.

First are a repeated reminder and a repeated caution. Repeated reminder: Readers, you can use of the Dream-Guided Meditation Model without learning how to interpret your dreams. Repeated caution: For those who are or have considered working with your dreams, if you have negative and fearful dreams, read Appendix B, Caveat on Bad and Worrisome Dreams by Edward Bruce Bynum, before you attempt to work alone with your dreams.

So now we present dreams that show how to still the thoughts. Stilling the thoughts is a pre-step to becoming aware of your still state in Stage Three.

Still Your Thoughts

One activity that thoughts can have a major impact on is meditation. Monkey mind is one way to symbolize rambling thoughts that interfere with meditation. The monkey mind dream came one night after rambling thoughts interfered with my meditation attempts.

DREAM: THE MONKEY MIND

During the dream *a monkey plays cards with me. There are problem-working cards and blank cards. The monkey only plays with the problem-working cards. He doesn't play with the blank cards.*

Problem-working cards, in the context of this dream, symbolize rambling thoughts. Blank cards symbolize spaces between thoughts, spaces between monkey mind thoughts.

The monkey, monkey mind, didn't play with the blank cards. He only played with the problem-working cards, the thoughts. He needed to still his thoughts, even for an instant. Then there would have been spaces in his thoughts. The message of this dream is: "When you meditate, at least some of the time, leave spaces in your thoughts."

Also in the dream, *the monkey and I stack up candles and flowers. Now and then the monkey slips an artificial flower into the stack.* Though I don't use candles and flowers for meditation, I know some meditation methods do use candles and flowers. When *the monkey slips an artificial flower into the stack*, the dream reveals I only imitated meditation, like artificial flowers only imitate their natural counterparts.

> **How to Use This Dream:** As much as you can, leave spaces between your thoughts, even for short instants. When you leave spaces in your thoughts you have the potential to become aware of your inner still state.
>
> Note: A way to still the thoughts fell into my mind one night when I had a deep desire to be still. Those words were: "Peace, peace, peace be still." Those words have since come at times to help me still my thoughts. Try it; it works.
>
> The next dream shows how to transcend negative emotions and negative thoughts. Use of the PMID model remains the way to unravel messages in meditation dreams at this point, offering amazing clarity when dreams can be connected to pre-dream events and thoughts, as this next dream demonstrates.

DREAM: USHER THE DOMINANT WOMAN AND THE OTHERS OUT OF THE CHURCH

I am standing at the door of the church and ushering the people out . . . I reach my arm out and signal for the row a woman and her companions are sitting in to exit first. The woman could be someone I disagreed with or have been angry with, but I am not feeling any anger toward her or disagreement with her now. I am graciously allowing her the privilege of being among the first to leave the church. I think of her as a dominant but elegant woman.

PMID Step 1: Connect your previous day (often the day before) events to the dream to discover the theme of this dream.

The night before this dream my husband and I watched a comedy television program that I generally enjoy, but this time the woman star was more absurd than usual and I felt angry about her actions. We watched other programs, and afterward I vowed, deeply vowed, I would shut these programs off, especially thoughts and emotions about the woman star of the comedy program, from interfering with my meditations and with my dreams.

PMID Step 2: Connect your previous day (often the day before) thoughts to your dream to detect which thoughts may have prompted this dream's responses. Write "I thought" statements and record when you thought them.

The night before this dream I had angry thoughts and emotions about the star on the comedy television program. I thought I could shut those thoughts off from interfering with my meditations and with my dreams. A thought-question this dream responds to is: "Have I successfully cleared my mind of angry thoughts and emotions?"

PMID Step 3: Select and define major words and phrases from your write-up of this dream to discover the dream's personalized meanings. The general definition for "phrases" as used in this step is "a string of words," which can be phrases, clauses, or whole sentences.

- **Standing at the door of a church:** Reflects my pre-dream affirmation for help with meditation. Though most of my meditations are at home, churches often symbolize meditation to me.
- **Dominant woman:** This is the star from the comedy TV program we watched during the evening. She portrays an elegant woman.
- **Signal for the row a woman and her companions are sitting in to exit first:** This indicates that I successfully cleared my mind of angry thoughts and emotions I had toward the star of the comedy TV program last night. The woman's companions symbolize the

other programs we watched last night that I vowed I would shut out of my mind.

PMID Step 4: Compare your emotions in your dream with your pre-dream, waking-life emotions to discover whether your waking-life emotions accurately reflect how you feel about the issue in this dream.

During the dream I feel no anger toward the dominant woman. Before this dream, after first feeling anger toward this actress, I changed those emotions by changing and stilling my thoughts.

PMID Step 5: Explore your dream for possible solutions to problems, including changing (or affirming) your thoughts, attitudes, or behaviors.

Readers, did you notice this dream is a response to my pre-sleep affirmation to keep thoughts and emotions, especially thoughts and emotions of the woman who touts herself to be elegant, from interfering with my meditations and with my dreams? During the dream "I am not feeling any anger toward her or disagreement with her now." Here the dream confirms my success to change pre-dream anger thoughts and emotions. It also shows what I did to change those thoughts: Calmly ushered dominant and mundane thoughts and emotions from the mind, ushering the dominant thoughts and emotions out first.

How to Use This Dream: Use the dream as inspiration that, yes, there is power to usher thoughts and emotions, dominant and mundane thoughts and emotions, out of the mind.

My need to still the thoughts continued in my dreams. A day or two before this next dream I read material about stilling the thoughts for meditation. Then, during meditation, I became especially aware of how difficult it is to still my thoughts.

DREAM: RESPONSES FROM BECOMING ESPECIALLY AWARE OF THE DIFFICULTY OF STILLING THE THOUGHTS THAT CROSS THE MIND

I am on a busload of people. The woman driver is waiting to turn across a busy interstate highway. She waits a long time for cars to clear before she crosses the highway. Then she crosses the highway and drives across the divider line and onto a very quiet, perhaps single-lane, road. I wonder why she waited so long to cross the highway. It seems to me she could have squeezed across the highway before now.

PMID Step 1: Connect your previous day (often the day before) events to the dream to discover the theme of this dream.

The night before this dream I read teachings about stilling the thoughts.

PMID Step 2: Connect your previous day (often the day before) thoughts to your dream to detect which thoughts may have prompted this dream's responses. Write "I thought" statements and record when you thought them.

The night before this dream I thought I understood the teachings I read about stilling the thoughts. A thought-question this dream responds to is: "Did I truly understand the teachings I read last night?"

PMID Step 3: Select and define major words and phrases from your write-up of this dream to discover the dream's personalized meanings. The general definition for "phrases" as used in this step is "a string of words," which can be phrases, clauses, or whole sentences.

- **Busload of people:** In the context of this dream, symbolic of the many thoughts that cross through people's minds.
- **Woman driver:** In the context of the whole dream, this fact is symbolic of a person who is in control of her thoughts. Women often symbolize the intuitive mode for both males and females.
- **Waiting to turn across a busy interstate highway:** This represents waiting for thoughts to become still.
- **Waits a long time for cars to clear before she crosses the highway:** Waiting for thoughts to clear from the mind can take a long time.
- **Drives across the divider line and onto a very quiet road:** This represents having crossed over from busy thoughts to a still mind.
- **Wonder why she waited so long to cross the highway:** This indicates that, at the time of this dream, I had slipped back from being aware of how long it takes to still my thoughts.
- **It seems to me she could have squeezed across the highway before now:** Dreams tell on us. Here the dream shows I was trying to still my thoughts without patient waiting.

During my dream I feel surprised the bus driver waited so long, that it takes so long to clear thoughts from the mind. In waking life the night before this dream I was impressed with teachings I had read about stilling the thoughts. This dream responds to those teachings and adds wisdom of its own. Beautiful. During my dream *It seems to me she could have squeezed across the highway before now*, which symbolizes that though I was impressed with the teachings I read last night and thought I understood them, I need to be more patient as I wait for my thoughts to clear. The answer to my thought-question, "Did I truly understand the teachings I read last night?" is "No. I didn't truly understand the teachings I read last night."

This next dream shows I do understand stillness quite well and yet have little understanding of the other teachings I studied the day before this dream.

DREAM: STAND STILL IS THE ONE MESSAGE THE STUDENTS UNDERSTAND

I am a substitute teacher, and I don't do a very good job with the material I am teaching. The material isn't something I know well. The students seem bored, are restless, and don't seem to be paying attention to what I am saying.

There are several paragraphs. At the beginning of each paragraph is a leading sentence or phrase to introduce different ideas.

Then one time I say, "Stand still and hear . . ." (On recall I'm uncertain what the end of the sentence is, but the words "stand still" are exactly what I said.) My husband is here and says something like, "That is the most important point." The students listen to this point, too.

Next, one student asks if it is break time. I look at the clock and see it is 2:00. Oh, my goodness. I have been talking for perhaps an hour and a half. Yes, it is time for a break.

PMID Step 1: Connect your previous day (often the day before) events to the dream to discover the theme of this dream.

Yesterday I studied some spirituality teachings that were new to me.

PMID Step 2: Connect your previous day (often the day before) thoughts to your dream to detect which thoughts may have prompted this dream's responses. Write "I thought" statements and record when you thought them.

As I studied those teachings I thought they could be of use and something to share with others. This dream responds to this thought-question: "Are these new teachings of use and something to share with others?"

PMID Step 3: Select and define major words and phrases from your write-up of this dream to discover the dream's personalized meanings. The general definition for "phrases" as used in this step is "a string of words," which can be phrases, clauses, or whole sentences.

- **Substitute teacher:** Substitute teachers likely have less command of the subject than do regular teachers. Here my dream shows I did not fully understand the new teachings I studied yesterday.

- **Students seem bored, are restless, and don't seem to be paying attention to what I am saying:** In the context of this dream, the students seeming to be bored shows that parts of the teachings I studied yesterday are ones I wouldn't do well in teaching to others.
- **Leading sentence or phrase is to introduce different ideas:** The format of the material was written well. However, as the dream shows, I didn't know parts of the material that well.
- **"Stand still":** Still your thoughts.
- **My husband is here and he says something like, "That is the most important point":** Still your thoughts is the most important point in the material I studied.
- **The students listen to this point, too:** This dream shows I am capable of teaching how to still the thoughts for meditation.
- **See it is 2:00:** This is representative of times when I "stood still." "Something" woke me at exactly 2:00 a.m., and I knew this "Something" was beyond my physical self.
- **Yes, it is time for a break:** Those times when I woke at 2:00 a.m. I knew it was special. Here I believe the special message is: "Take a break from studying most of these new teachings."

PMID Step 4: Compare your emotions in your dream with your pre-dream, waking-life emotions to discover whether your waking-life emotions accurately reflect how you feel about the issue in this dream.

As my dream shows, my waking-life enthusiasm for the new teachings was inaccurate regarding how I truly feel about most of those teachings.

PMID Step 5: Explore your dream for possible solutions to problems, including changing (or affirming) your thoughts, attitudes, or behaviors.

Notice, during the dream "stand still" (still your thoughts) is the one message that attracts the students' attention. It is the one point in the new teachings I read yesterday that I am capable of teaching well.

(Note: I purposely omit the name of the teachings in question because they are obviously helpful for some people.)

PMID Step 6: Explore your dream for family and other relationships shown or implicated in the dream.

My husband is in this dream. My longtime respect for and reactions to his characteristic notice of important points, and his cautions regarding some of those important points, helps me value his comment during this dream. There is only one important point for me in the new-to-me spirituality teachings: Stand still, be still: Still your thoughts.

This next dream shows success in stilling the thoughts when the meditator lets the train of thoughts pass by.

DREAM: STAND STILL AND LET THE TRAIN OF THOUGHTS PASS BY

I am standing at a train crossing as the train is passing by. The words "stand still" run through my mind. I am not afraid of getting in front of the train, though.

PMID Step 1: Connect your previous day (often the day before) events to the dream to discover the theme of this dream.

At the time of this dream, I am having good success with stilling my thoughts for meditation.

PMID Step 2: Connect your previous day (often the day before) thoughts to your dream to detect which thoughts may have prompted this dream's responses. Write "I thought" statements and record when you thought them.

Last night when I went to bed I realized I was in a meditative state. Then I continued with stilling my thoughts.

PMID Step 3: Select and define major words and phrases from your write-up of this dream to discover the dream's personalized meanings. The general definition for "phrases" as used in this step is "a string of words," which can be phrases, clauses, or whole sentences.

- **Standing at a train crossing as the train is passing by:** Here, I believe, my dream act symbolizes that I waited for the train of mental thoughts to pass by.
- **Words "stand still" run through my mind:** Here, I believe, the dream calls attention to the meditative state I was in before I meditated last night. I had stilled my thoughts; I had let the train of mental thoughts pass on by.

Success with stilling the thoughts, yes!

Listen

Now we present dreams that show how to listen to become aware of the still state. Listening is a pre-step to becoming aware of the still state of Stage Three.

DREAM: LISTENING AND PRACTICE ARE ESSENTIAL FOR SUCCESSFUL MEDITATION

I'm at my piano teacher's house. I hear her say, "If you haven't practiced, then don't play today." (I had been lax in meditations.) *I play anyway. I take some of my piano pieces out and flip through them to find an easy one to play.*

My teacher plays one of my piano pieces. The teacher says how beautiful my piece is. It is one of my music pieces. I realize the teacher's playing is beautiful, but I want to play my piece myself instead of listening to the teacher play my piece.

PMID Step 1: Connect your previous day (often the day before) events to the dream to discover the theme of this dream.

I have been reading and studying wonderful writings of one of my favorite authors. I have read the book before, but this time I am able to study it in a way I've never done before. It resonates much with me. Yet, now I have not been experiencing the depth of meditation that I had been though studying and dream work are going well for me.

PMID Step 2: Connect your previous day (often the day before) thoughts to your dream to detect which thoughts may have prompted this dream's responses. Write "I thought" statements and record when you thought them.

Yesterday after reading the inspiring teachings, I wondered about my lack of success with meditation, though studying and dream work are going well for me. A possible thought-question this dream responds to is: "Why my lack of success with deep meditation now?"

PMID Step 3: Select and define major dream phrases and symbols from your write-up of this dream to discover the dream's personalized meanings. The general definition for "phrases" as used in this step is "a string of words," which can be phrases, clauses, or whole sentences.

- **At my piano teacher's house:** The piano is a musical instrument. Music in dreams in this book often symbolizes successful meditation.
- **"If you haven't practiced, then don't play today":** I have been lax in dedicating myself to meditation and so attempts to meditate will likely be ineffective.
- **Play anyway:** This dream tells on me. My dreams do that. The dream shows I have been attempting to meditate without dedicated practice.
- **I flip through my piano pieces to find an easy one to play:** I attempt to find an easy way to meditate without having practiced.
- **My teacher:** This is my inner teacher; I am being taught from within my own being.
- **My teacher plays one of my piano pieces:** Successful results from listening during meditation.
- **The teacher says how beautiful my piece is:** A sense of peaceful beauty results from successful listening during meditation.

- **I want to play my piece myself:** Meditation from a surface level, which is my choice when I haven't practiced. Even inspiring readings do not replace the need for dedicated practice of listening.
- **Instead of listening to the teacher play my piece:** Instead of listening, I've been trying to meditate from a surface level of contemplation.

How to Use This Dream: Remember what the teacher in this dream says when she plays one of my pieces. She says how beautiful it is. Listen, instead of depending on surface-level meditations, or even inspiring readings, for effective meditation.

This next dream is an example of meditating from a surface level. The dream even describes a surface level of meditation as a *third- and fourth-grade* level of meditation.

DREAM: REMINDED TO MEDITATE WITH THE FULL DREAM-GUIDED MEDITATION MODEL

I am in an unfamiliar classroom somewhat like the third- and fourth-grade room at my childhood grade school. Students are doing meditation exercises. Sally (pseudonym) *is standing and doing some sort of* [physical] *exercise.*

Sally comes to me and says she just doesn't understand how to meditate this way. She asks me to help her with meditation.

I am concerned about doing meditation myself and I don't feel very much like I can help her. Yet, I do think of the meditation I was guided to write, but haven't used much myself lately. I tell her about that process.

PMID Step 1: Connect your previous day (often the day before) events to the dream to discover the theme of this dream.

During the night I worked with meditation before I fell asleep and dreamed this dream.

PMID Step 2: Connect your previous day (often the day before) thoughts to your dream to detect which thoughts may have prompted this dream's responses. Write "I thought" statements and record when you thought them.

I have been thinking my meditations are more on the outer instead of on the inner. This resulting dream translates those thoughts into a thought-question: "Have my meditations been more on the outer instead of on the inner?" My personalized definitions of phrases, even whole sentences from the dream, answer that question.

PMID Step 3: Select and define major words and phrases from your write-up of this dream to discover the dream's personalized meanings.

The general definition for "phrases" as used in this step is "a string of words," which can be phrases, clauses, or whole sentences.

- **Unfamiliar classroom:** There is something to learn that I'm unfamiliar with at the time of this dream.
- **Somewhat like the third and fourth grade room at my childhood grade school:** I'm trying to meditate at an elementary level.
- **Sally is standing and doing some sort of (physical) exercise:** Perhaps this means I only paid attention to the quieting my body part of meditation when I meditated at night.
- **Don't feel very much like I can help her (Sally):** This shows my lack of confidence in my ability to move to deeper level meditations at the time of this dream.
- **Yet, I do think of the meditation I was guided to write, but haven't used much myself lately:** The dream shows I've gone away from the Dream-Guided Meditation Model.

PMID Step 4: Compare your emotions in your dream with your pre-dream, waking-life emotions to discover whether your waking-life emotions accurately reflect how you feel about the issue in this dream.

During my dream I feel concerned about my ability to meditate and I feel a lack of ability to help Sally. Those are nearly the same concerns I had in waking life the day before this dream.

PMID Step 5: Explore your dream for possible solutions to problems, including changing (or affirming) your thoughts, attitudes, or behaviors.

My pre-dream thought-question was: "Have my meditations been more on the outer instead of on the inner?" The answer: Yes.

PMID Step 6: Explore your dream for family and other relationships shown or implicated in the dream.

Sally, in my limited experiences with her, is usually a surface-level thinking type person. My reactions to her as a surface-level thinking person help me realize her part in this dream. Her presence shows I'm meditating on a surface or outer level.

How I Used This Dream: After I woke from the dream I realized what the dream meant. Then I meditated by using the full Dream-Guided Meditation Model. Later in the morning I suddenly realized how inward and how peaceful I felt. I knew it was from the meditation and having stilled my thoughts and listened.

The next dreams center on becoming aware of the still state. Study these dreams for insights on becoming aware of the still state within your mind.

Become Aware of Your Still State

As the dreams in this chapter reveal, there is a capacity, a stillness in our minds, beyond words and thoughts. Computers symbolize the mind for me because of their abundant capacities.

DREAM: TO ACCESS DEEPER LEVELS DURING MEDITATION, USE THE DREAM-GUIDED MEDITATION MODEL

It is dusky. I am working at a computer. I notice some noise as I turn the computer on. It does this more than once.

Then I see the screen shows a circle for the "A" drive and has a little bar of notes under the bar. The computer plays the music of those notes to signify access to the "A" drive. I know that is what the sound means.

There are other drives; when I can access them the screen will play the music score under them. There are two other circles visible. The one most clear is the E drive. There is a music score under it, but it is faint and doesn't play the music; it just has the noise.

I recall there is a procedure to set these up. I have done the procedure before, and then I have access to several drives. I'll take time to look in the instruction manual to see how to set that up again.

PMID Step 1: Connect your previous day (often the day before) events to the dream to discover the theme of this dream.

During the night I worked with the Dream-Guided Meditation Model. When I was still in Stage One, Quiet the Whole Body, awareness came of "Oh, Infinite Mind is here during this part of the meditation, too." Even then I didn't make progress. Then I fell asleep, though I had resolved to finish the meditation. A possible theme of this dream is: "Beyond quieting the body."

PMID Step 2: Connect your previous day (often the day before) thoughts to your dream to detect which thoughts may have prompted this dream's responses. Write "I thought" statements and record when you thought them.

A couple nights ago I thought about letting myself be affected by other people's thoughts and actions during the day, but night is the time I have to myself for my thoughts. A possible thought-question is: "Does my time for myself with my thoughts impede my ability to become aware of the still state?"

PMID Step 3: Select and define major words and phrases from your write-up of this dream to discover the dream's personalized meanings.

The general definition for "phrases" as used in this step is "a string of words," which can be phrases, clauses, or whole sentences.

- **Dusky:** This represents something in this dream I don't see, don't understand clearly.
- **Working at a computer:** In the context of this dream, the computer symbolizes my mind during meditation.
- **Screen shows a circle for the "A" drive and has a little bar of notes under the bar:** In the context of this dream, this likely represents success with beginning the meditation.
- **Computer plays the music of those notes to signify access to the "A" drive:** Music in my meditation dreams often symbolizes successful meditation.
- **Are other drives; when I can access them the screen will play the music score under them:** This is a reference to increasing depth of meditation.
- **Are two other circles visible:** This represents the potential for increasing depths of meditation.
- **One most clear is the E drive:** In the context of this dream, I believe the E stands for a depth I was unable to reach during meditation last night.
- **There is a music score under it (the E drive), but it is faint and doesn't play the music; it just has the noise:** No music, just noise, symbolizes I was unsuccessful in achieving deep meditation. This reflects last night when I fell asleep during my meditation.
- **Recall there is a procedure to set these up:** This setup procedure could be, must be, the need to still the thoughts and listen to be able to complete the full procedure of the Dream-Guided Meditation Model, including become aware of the still state.
- **Have done it before and then I have access to several drives**: I have been successful with using the full Dream-Guided Meditation Model before. Then I had "access to several drives," meaning I relaxed into a deep meditative state.

PMID Step 5: Explore your dream for possible solutions to problems, including changing (or affirming) your thoughts, attitudes, or behaviors.

The answer to my thought question "Does my time for myself with my thoughts impede my ability to become aware of the still state" is yes. As revealed in the dream, "*I'll take time to look in the instruction manual and see how to set that up again.*" Good idea! The solution in this dream is to still my thoughts, even "my own thoughts" beyond thoughts about other people. The answer in this dream is study the full Dream-Guided Meditation Model for how to set up the still state.

How I Used This Dream: After I woke from the dream I realized what the dream meant. Then I used the full Dream-Guided Meditation Model given to me in a dream: Quiet Your Whole Body, Slow Your Breath, and Still Your Thoughts and Listen to Become Aware of Your Still State. Later in the morning I suddenly realized how inward and how peaceful I felt. I knew it was from the meditation.

Reminder: Readers, I repeat—inward peaceful feelings may occur only infrequently. Whether inward peaceful feelings occur during your meditations, be grateful for whatever success you gain. Feeling discouraged (as I have at times) interferes with meditations.

Beyond realizing the far reaches of the mind are needed to become aware of your still state, there is still one more need: Be patient to stay in the meditative state.

DREAM: STAY IN THE MEDITATIVE STATE AND WAIT PATIENTLY!

I am at a doctor's office. The nurse has done something. I sit on a bench and wait for the next procedure. The doctor comes and wraps a rubber band around my arm, does something else, and then leaves. I don't notice the rubber band until later.

After the doctor leaves, I return to the nurse's area. Then I realize, "Oh, I have this rubber band on my arm, but I didn't wait until the doctor put the needle in my arm." I laugh and tell the nurse.

The doctor comes to the nurse's area and looks for me. So I go back and sit on the bench in the doctor's office. I know it is late in the day and I am one of the last ones to be taken care of; it is likely I am the last one. I wait, but the doctor doesn't come back.

PMID Step 1: Connect your previous day (often the day before) events to the dream to discover the theme of this dream.

During the very early morning I woke and was restless. After struggling a long time to get back to sleep, I decided, "Well, I'll meditate." I did work at it, but I became impatient and frustrated when I didn't achieve a deep meditation.

PMID Step 2: Connect your previous day (often the day before) thoughts to your dream to detect which thoughts may have prompted this dream's responses. Write "I thought" statements and record when you thought them.

When I didn't achieve a deep meditation, I thought about my need to be in a spirituality consciousness for the work ahead of me with dreams.

A thought-question this dream responds to is: "What do I need to do to achieve spirituality consciousness for the work ahead of me with dreams?"

PMID Step 3: Select and define major words and phrases from your write-up of this dream to discover the dream's personalized meanings. The general definition for "phrases" as used in this step is "a string of words," which can be phrases, clauses, or whole sentences.

- **Rubber band around my arm:** This is preparation for some kind of procedure, which is meditation in this context.
- **Don't notice the rubber band until later:** I left meditation and didn't realize the potential to be achieved had I continued.
- **Doctor comes out to the nurse's room for me:** In the context of this dream, this represents inspirations for meditation continued in my mind.
- **One of the last ones to be taken care of:** The time I woke was near time to get up. Thus in a sense it was my last chance for meditation before getting up.
- **Wait but the doctor doesn't come back:** I did begin a short meditation, but I fell back asleep and dreamed this dream.

PMID Step 4: Compare your emotions in your dream with your pre-dream, waking-life emotions to discover whether your waking-life emotions accurately reflect how you feel about the issue in this dream.

During my dream I laugh when I realize I hadn't waited long enough for the doctor. (Symbolically, I didn't wait patiently to still my thoughts and listen to become aware of my still state, which contrasts with my pre-dream yearning for successful meditation.) My amusement during my dream makes me wonder how deeply I yearned for successful meditation before I fell asleep and dreamed this dream. A very humbling revelation.

This dream's response to my pre-dream thoughts on my need to achieve spirituality consciousness for the work ahead of me with dreams is: "Stay with the meditation process and wait patiently!" Patient waiting is paramount for successful meditation. How many times must dreams remind me before I consistently wait for the still state during meditation?

Though our meditative preference is for deep relaxation into a still state, we can achieve a level of success when we avoid frustrating emotions, as the next dream shows. Notice the symbolism in the dream: *I don't seem to feel concerned* when *now and then a fish runs into one of my legs* and *now and then one of my feet slips off a ledge, but I don't seem to feel concerned about that either*.

DREAM: CONFIDENCE THAT YESTERDAY'S SECOND MEDITATION WAS DEEP THOUGH COULD HAVE BEEN DEEPER

I am walking on an underwater ledge. I am quite happy as I walk. There are fish in the water. Now and then a fish runs into one of my legs, but I don't seem to feel concerned about it or mind it. Now and then one of my feet slips off the ledge, but I don't seem to feel concerned about that either.

PMID Step 1: Connect your previous day (often the day before) events to the dream to discover the theme of this dream.

Yesterday I read in Corey (2009) that systems perspectives of counseling have the possibility of being called "the fourth force" of counseling. I realized, "Yes, that is what the Personalized Method for Interpreting Dreams (PMID) is; it is a systems approach to counseling."

Then I spent much time trying to create a new title for a book I am writing; I wanted to include the systems perspective to fit with the fourth force conception of relationship systems. After unsuccessful attempts to develop a new title, I began my after-work meditation early in hopes of inspiration for a new title; but I became restless so I stopped without going into the longer meditation.

When I went back to meditate later, I had only begun when an idea popped into my mind: "Tell the colleague I had asked to draft some pages about cognitive therapy to instead draft some pages about systems perspectives, the fourth force." Though it had been a couple of months since the colleague had contacted me, he responded immediately. Without knowing of my change of mind, he had already drafted some pages about systems perspectives and planned to send those pages to me on the weekend.

PMID Step 2: Connect your previous day (often the day before) thoughts to your dream to detect which thoughts may have prompted this dream's responses. Write "I thought" statements and record when you thought them.

As shown under PMID Step 1, "When I went back to meditate later, I had only begun when an idea popped into my mind: 'Tell the colleague I had asked to draft some pages about cognitive therapy to instead draft some pages about systems perspectives, the fourth force.'"

PMID Step 3: Select and define major words and phrases from your write-up of this dream to discover the dream's personalized meanings. The general definition for "phrases" as used in this step is "a string of words," which can be phrases, clauses, or whole sentences.

- **Underwater ledge:** A symbolic meaning of water is spirituality, which connects to yesterday's meditations.
- **Fish in the water:** A universal meaning is: "The size, color, and looks of a fish often represent the dreamer's present spiritual evolution, as does the size of the body of water" (Boushahla and Reidel-Geubtner, 1992). Here, it means yesterday's successful meditation (the second time I meditated) as symbolized by fish in the water.
- **Now and then a fish runs into my leg:** This shows my current support (universal meaning of leg) of my "present spiritual evolution" has some discrepancies.
- **Now and then one of my feet slips off the ledge:** This is another sign that my current understanding of my "present spiritual evolution" has some discrepancies. A universal meaning of feet is understanding.

PMID Step 4: Compare your emotions in your dream with your pre-dream, waking-life emotions to discover whether your waking-life emotions accurately reflect how you feel about the issue in this dream.

This dream symbolizes the emotions I felt during my second meditation. During the dream I feel quite happy as I walked on the ledge, and I don't seem to feel concerned about or mind it when fish run into my leg or when I slip off the ledge. Though, as the dream symbolizes, my current support and understanding of my present spiritual evolution have some discrepancies, I still had a successful meditation that resulted in a helpful insight. In waking life during my second meditation I felt grateful for the idea that popped into my mind: "Tell the colleague I had asked to draft some pages about cognitive therapy to instead draft some pages about systems perspectives, the fourth force."

How to Use This Dream: Remember, there is success with meditation when the meditator keeps from becoming drawn into frustrated emotions. Feeling discouraged (as I have at times) interferes with successful meditation.

The day before this next dream I pressed myself to accomplish more work projects than I had time to do. Then during the night a dream counseled me on how I could have calmed myself and been more productive.

DREAM: TAKE TIME FOR MEDITATION: IT IS WORTH $1,000 IN CALM WISDOM

I am a worker in an office, an observer; that may be my primary role here. There are two young men who stay in rooms in a building not far from the *office. That is where they live. It seems I don't think it unusual, but later a man in the office tells me this one fellow is brilliant, that he earns $1,000 an hour. So they have great respect for him. This young man is somewhat like one of my former colleagues.*

Then I am sitting at a desk as I watch a woman who reminds me of a professor I know. Another woman sits on the other side of the professor as they both work on typewriters. The professor is the primary one I am focused on in the dream. Someone has given her some handwritten material that she is almost in a panic to get copied into the typewriter.

I watch her as she does this. She takes out another typewriter, a smaller typewriter with a cover on it. I assume she uses it as the other one runs out.

The woman beside her takes out a second smaller typewriter with a cover on it. It seems like the professor uses three typewriters altogether.

Later I watch the professor as she is at another table and continues to work as fast as she can to get this copied. I am thinking this is something she needs to get done before the end of this day and it is to meet a due date for a customer.

The professor says she cannot read this writing very well. I look at the writing and wonder why she feels so confused. The writing looks relatively clear to me.

PMID Step 1: Connect your previous day (often the day before) events to the dream to discover the theme of this dream.

Yesterday I worked on three typing projects for my husband, which included using both of our computers. I also worked on a book in progress. A few days prior I told my husband when I was a secretary, I prided myself on how fast I could work but now it takes a lot of time to accomplish the kind of work I do.

Last night I had a few irregular heartbeats. This is the first that has happened in a long, long time—several years.

PMID Step 2: Connect your previous day (often the day before) thoughts to your dream to detect which thoughts may have prompted this dream's responses. Write "I thought" statements and record when you thought them.

Yesterday, I thought about a professor I know (the professor in this dream) because this is the first week of a change of pace for her, from vacation time back to her professorship work.

PMID Step 3: Select and define major words and phrases from your write-up of this dream to discover the dream's personalized meanings. The general definition for "phrases" as used in this step is "a string of words, which can be phrases, clauses, or whole sentences.

- **Am a worker in an office:** This is my office where I was yesterday when I worked on three projects.
- **An observer; that may be my primary role here:** My primary role in this dream is to observe the suggestion this dream brings.
- **Two young men:** In the context of this dream this represents two aspects of meditation. One is discipline to meditate, and the other is the result of successful meditation, peace and inner calm.
- **Rooms in a building not far from the office:** In the context of this dream, the room where I meditate is "not far from" my office here in our home.
- **Where they live:** Where my meditations come alive is the room where I meditate. That is where this dream shows to go to calm myself.
- **Seems I don't think it unusual:** A designated location for meditation is typical—at least it is for me.
- **One fellow is brilliant, that he earns $1,000 an hour**: The brilliant fellow represents success to attain peace and inner calm during meditation. If I had become peaceful and calm the day before the dream I could have symbolically earned $1,000 an hour in productive work. See below for my definition of "Young man is somewhat like one of my former colleagues."
- **Have great respect for him:** Here my dream reminds me of the respect I have for calmness and deep focus during meditation.
- **Young man is somewhat like one of my former colleagues:** This former colleague's work style was calmness and deep focus.
- **Sitting at a desk as I watch a woman who reminds me of a professor I know:** I thought about this woman yesterday because it is the first week of a change of pace for her, from vacation back to her professorship work.
- **Another woman sits on the other side of the professor as they both work on typewriters:** This demonstrates the work I did on two computers yesterday.
- **Professor is the primary one I am focused on in the dream:** She represents the "change of pace" work I did yesterday when I worked on more projects than usual.
- **Someone has given her some handwritten material that she is almost in a panic to get copied into the typewriter:** These are the shorthand notes I had written for my book in progress.
- **Takes out another typewriter, a smaller typewriter with a cover on it:** This could represent when I went to our second computer, a smaller computer, took the cover off, and began to use it.

- **Woman beside her takes out a second typewriter with a cover on it:** This woman could represent when I began secretarial work for my husband yesterday.
- **Thinking this is something she needs to get done before the end of this day and it is to meet a due date for a customer:** That's what I wanted to do with the secretarial work I did for my husband yesterday. I wanted to complete it before bedtime. My husband (the customer) suggested I go to bed instead; I felt tired, and so I did go to bed.
- **Professor says she cannot read this writing very well:** Yesterday when I typed from my shorthand notes for my book in progress—granted I was hurrying then—I was surprised my notes didn't seem as clear as they had when I was writing them.
- **Look at the writing and wonder why she feels so confused because the writing looks relatively clear to me:** In waking life, after this dream, as I looked at my shorthand notes in a calm concentrated way I saw they were clear.

This dream shows why I felt tense yesterday; instead of using meditation to calm myself, I pressed onward to accomplish more work projects than is usual for me. Early in the dream I am shown a brilliant way to have attained peace and inner calm to accomplish the work ahead of me.

The brilliant way to attain peace and inner calm is meditation. In the dream *a man in the office tells me this one fellow is brilliant, that he earns $1,000 an hour. So they have great respect for him.* I do have great respect for the peace and inner calm derived from meditation. When I successfully use the Dream-Guided Meditation Model to quiet my whole body, slow my breath, and still my thoughts and listen to become aware of my still state, I do attain peace and inner calm.

Summary of Chapter 4

This chapter explains and expands on the third stage of the Dream-Guided Meditation Model. Deep immersion in Quiet Your Whole Body (Stage One) and Slow Your Breath (Stage Two) moves the meditator toward Stage Three of the model, Still Your Thoughts and Listen to Become Aware of Your Still State. The still state originates from the words "Arizona State" in the Dream-Guided Meditation Model presented in Chapter 1 of this book, where "zona state" is translated as the still state. In this chapter we learned that thoughts often interfere with the meditator's ability to become aware of the still state. Thus, several dreams are included that show how to still the thoughts on the way to becoming aware of the still state. The next chapter demonstrates the highest potential from successful use of the full Dream-Guided Meditated Model.

References

Boushahla, J., & Reidel-Geubtner, V. (1992). *The dream dictionary*. New York: Berkley.

Corey, G. (2009). *Theory and practice of counseling and psychotherapy* (8th ed.). Belmont, CA: Brooks/Cole.

5 Potential Result of Using the Dream-Guided Meditation Model

Become Conscious of the Higher Self Potential within Your Being, a Presence in All Human Beings

Readers, we have just completed the full three-stage Dream-Guided Meditation Model presented in Chapter 1 and clarified in subsequent chapters. Before we begin this chapter on the potential result from use of the Dream-Guided Meditation Model, refresh your minds by using the model: Quiet Your Whole Body, Slow Your Breath, and Still Your Thoughts and Listen to Become Aware of Your Still State.

And please remember: Just as life is a journey, so is meditation a journey. When we overlook benefits that can accrue from becoming absorbed in each stage of the Dream-Guided Meditation Model, and instead focus only on the potential outcome over time, we deprive ourselves of the benefits that could be gained from each stage in our meditation journey. Stages one and two of the Dream-Guided Meditation Model (Quiet Your Whole Body and Slow Your Breath) can relax you for the activities ahead. Stage three of the Meditation Model (Still Your Thoughts and Listen to Become Aware of Your Still State) can bring intuitive knowing, peacefulness, and even feelings of love at times. Yet, whatever results you experience, keep from pressing yourself. Be grateful for benefits you gain from dedicated meditation.

Over time your dedicated use of the full model may lead you into awareness beyond your usual common thoughts, to consciousness of your Higher Self.

This chapter presents dreams that picture results of awareness beyond common mental thoughts. That awareness is shown symbolically in one dream as the Fourth Square, and is shown in a second dream as the Higher Self beyond words and thoughts. Recall from the Dream-Guided Meditation Model (Chapter 1) that the Higher Self potential present in each human being seemed a possible result from success with the model. I believe the Higher Self potential present in each human being is reflected in the below dream when I say, "Infinite Mind and mind are the same," words I've not said during waking life.

DREAM: DEDICATED STUDENT CAUSES ME TO SAY MORE THAN I'D PLANNED (INFINITE MIND AND MIND ARE THE SAME. INFINITE MIND IS THE FOURTH SQUARE)

I am teaching a small class. It is dusky. The class members are all sitting in the front half of the room.

I know one fellow understands more than the others understand. He is quiet, though. As he comprehends, I go further and further, covering more than I'd planned. He seems like Kyle Hancock (a pseudonym), *but he isn't Kyle Hancock.*

Referring to four squares that I put on the board, I say, "To me Infinite Mind and mind are the same thing. Infinite Mind is the Fourth Square that I wasn't going to speak of." Kyle Hancock seems to understand at least slightly.

PMID Step 1: Connect your previous day (often the day before) events to the dream to discover the theme of this dream.

The night before this dream, my husband and I saw a television advertisement about a product being available all hours of the day and night. The advertisers emphasized their point by stating that Einstein, Beethoven, and others did their work during the night.

PMID Step 2: Connect your previous day (often the day before) thoughts to your dream to detect which thoughts may have prompted this dream's responses. Write "I thought" statements and record when you thought them.

After the advertisement about Einstein, Beethoven, and others' night work, I thought, "That is how it is when I am awake during the night and do my 'quiet times'" (a term I've used at times for meditation).

PMID Step 3: Select and define major words and phrases from your write-up of this dream to discover the dream's personalized meanings. The general definition for "phrases" as used in this step is "a string of words," which can be phrases, clauses, or whole sentences.

- **Dusky:** There is something in the dream I do not see or understand clearly.
- **Class members sit in the front half of the room:** This reflects the actual setting of my small class of advanced students; they sit in the front half of the room.
- **Fourth Square:** This is the fourth dimension beyond common thoughts, the third dimension being common thoughts.
- **Go further and further, covering more than I'd planned:** Knowledge from some capacity of the mind in the fourth dimension, or from above the limited dimensions of conscious thought.

- **To me Infinite Mind and mind are the same thing:** I believe the word "mind" (with a lowercase "m") symbolizes the Higher Self potential in each human being. (In waking life I have not said Infinite Mind and mind are the same.)

PMID Step 5: Explore your dream for possible solutions to problems, including changing (or affirming) your thoughts, attitudes, or behaviors.

The dream shows a way to come into knowing on the fourth dimension beyond words and conscious thoughts. It is by being so mentally dedicated to some pursuit of knowledge that information beyond conscious thoughts falls into the mind.

PMID Step 6: Explore your dream for family and other relationships shown or implicated in the dream to discover whether this dream reflects your reactions during earlier experiences with your family or other major relationships.

Kyle Hancock is the major relationship in this dream. In my view, he succeeds beyond his natural abilities because he dedicates himself to doing whatever activity he undertakes. This dream uses Kyle Hancock to represent the dedication it takes to go beyond mental awareness to consciousness of the "Fourth Square," to awareness of "Infinite Mind and mind are the same."

This next dream uses the words "Higher Self Consciousness," which, for me, mean the same as the word "mind" (with a lowercase "m") shown in the above "*Dedicated Student Causes Me to Say More Than I'd Planned (Infinite Mind and mind are the same. Infinite Mind is the Fourth Square*) dream.

DREAM: HIGHER SELF CONSCIOUSNESS IS BEYOND WORDS AND THOUGHTS

I am standing outside the door to a room. There is a woman who reads a question that seems to be from a radio or television program. It doesn't seem I am on the program . . .

The question is about . . . Higher Self Consciousness. The woman asks me what I think. I know in my mind's eye it seems I have answered this for myself very well. I say something like, "Well, I will try to put it in words as I understand it." My husband is standing near as he encourages me to respond, not in words, it seems, but he encourages me.

I explain that Higher Self Consciousness is beyond words and thoughts. The words I say during my dream are really quite fine, but I do not have complete recall as I type the dream.

There is a man here who is belligerent regarding what I have said. He says the mind has to stay at a lower level. I explain if one's mind is to stay at a lower level, it is not Higher Self Consciousness because the Higher Self is not conscious to the human mind at that level; the man understands.

PMID Step 1: Connect your previous day (often the day before) events to the dream to discover the theme of this dream.

Yesterday and last night I read several pages about what some call "the dark night of the soul." My understanding from those readings was dark night experiences are really leading people to what, for me, means their Higher Self potentials.

PMID Step 2: Connect your previous day (often the day before) thoughts to your dream to detect which thoughts may have prompted this dream's responses. Write "I thought" statements and record when you thought them.

Last night I thought about and wondered if my understanding of the material I read about "dark night" experiences can really lead people to what, for me, means their Higher Self potentials. A possible thought-question this dream responds to is: "Do negative dark night experiences really lead people to awareness of their Higher Selves?"

PMID Step 3: Select and define major words and phrases from your write-up of this dream to discover the dream's personalized meanings. The general definition for "phrases" as used in this step is "a string of words," which can be phrases, clauses, or whole sentences:

- **Standing outside the door to a room:** In the context of this dream, I am outside as if a listener to the teachings in the book I read yesterday.
- **Woman who reads a question that seems to be from a radio or television program:** I believe this woman could represent my intuitive level of thinking (I subscribe to the symbolism of intuition as female thinking regardless of gender).
- **Doesn't seem I am on the program:** The "program," the dark night of the soul teachings I read last night, do not apply to my path.
- **Question is about . . . Higher Self Consciousness:** This connects to the dream that brought the Dream-Guided Meditation Model (Chapter 1). In that dream, after the meditation model is presented, there is "*one word that . . . I realize symbolizes the Higher Self potential present in all persons.*"
- **Know in my mind's eye it seems I have answered this for myself very well:** A conception my dream shows I do know. Higher Self

Consciousness could connect to "have answered this for myself" as it ties to the Dream-Guided Meditation Model (Chapter 1).

- **My husband . . . encourages me to respond, but not in words it seems:** My husband is a quiet source of encouragement to my aspirations.
- **I explain that Higher Self Consciousness is beyond words and thoughts:** This is my dreaming mind's explanation of Higher Self Consciousness. The experience is beyond words and thoughts.
- **Man who is belligerent regarding what I have said:** This is an adverse response to my explanation that Higher Self Consciousness is beyond words and thoughts. The belligerent man could be my logical reasoning thoughts that perhaps what I read about the dark night as a way to awareness of the Higher Self potential in every human is a teaching I should follow. (I subscribe to the concept of masculine as symbolic of logical reasoning regardless of gender.)
- **Says the mind has to stay at a lower level:** When I think from my logical reasoning level, I consider rational assessment as the only way I can conceive meaning.
- **Explain if one's mind is to stay at a lower level, it is not Higher Self Consciousness because the Higher Self is not conscious to the human mind at that level:** This is beautiful and amazing substantiation that the dreaming mind brings to us such upper-level insights.
- **Man understands:** This represents that when shown specific upper-level insights, the logical thinking level of the mind comprehends.

My husband's quiet encouragement is shown in this dream. My current and earlier reactions to his unspoken support give me confidence to share my dream's explanation: "If one's mind is to stay at a lower level, it is not Higher Self Consciousness."

How to Use This Dream: Realize the Higher Self potential brings upper-level insights beyond our common thoughts.

Summary of Chapter 5

This chapter supports Higher Self presence in all human beings. In one dream, *Dedicated Student Causes Me to Say More Than I'd Planned (Infinite Mind and mind are the same. Infinite Mind is the Fourth Square)*, the word "mind" (with a lowercase "m") is interpreted as symbolic of the Higher Self potential in each human. The fourth dimension is beyond common thoughts. One way to come into knowing on the fourth dimension is by being so mentally dedicated to some pursuit of knowledge that information beyond conscious thoughts falls into the mind.

Section B

When and Where to Meditate

6 When to Meditate

Now that we have the full meditation model and potential result of using the Dream-Guided Meditation Model, it is time to focus on when to meditate. In our busy lives we wonder just when we can dedicate ourselves to taking time for meditation. Readers, during our busiest days there usually—likely always—is time to meditate. Why? Because successful meditation can bring calm wisdom for completing the day's activities. See Chapter 4 and the dream *Take Time for Meditation: It is Worth $1,000 in Calm Wisdom*.

Times to meditate suggested in this chapter are morning, noontime, after work, and any time you feel led to do so. Those are dream-guided meditation times for this writer. You may find those times productive for you as well. Begin with meditation for guidance every morning.

DREAM: MEDITATE FOR GUIDANCE EVERY MORNING

I am walking with others on our way to work. Along the way is a church. I drop out of the line for a short stop at the church before going on to work.

> **PMID Step 3:** Select and define major words and phrases from your write-up of this dream to discover the dream's personalized meanings. The general definition for "phrases" as used in this step is "a string of words," which can be phrases, clauses, or whole sentences.

- **On our way to work:** This indicates preparation for the day's work.
- **Along the way is a church:** The meaning of churches for me from early childhood has been as a place to worship. After I learned about meditation, churches began to appear as symbols for meditation, though I most often meditate at home.

- **Short stop at the church before going on to work:** This represents a brief meditation before beginning the day's activities.

This dream's suggestion is to meditate every morning. A "short stop" for a ten-minute meditation is so peaceful for me that I rarely miss this morning refresher.

Noontime is another time to meditate. My regular noontime meditation is one I began several years ago. I meditate for, "Peace and love and oneness and joy and light in the hearts and minds and souls of all the peoples of the world." The following dream affirms there are benefits from taking noontime meditations, relaxing noontime meditations, even without reaching the meditation depth desired.

DREAM: RELAXING NOONTIME MEDITATIONS

I go to a store and ask a favorite clerk for a toothpaste product. I see the clerks as they take relaxing noontime meditations.

There is a woman clerk I especially like. I desire for her to be with her child, or perhaps an adult, at least someone she loves, during the noontime meditations. Then I see her sitting in something like a windowsill. She is smiling and visiting with another woman, perhaps a clerk. She isn't with this loved person, but she is smiling and taking time to relax. So I do feel pleased for her.

PMID Step 1: Connect your previous day (often the day before) events to the dream to discover the theme of this dream.

Yesterday it was 12:00 noon when I finished putting materials away after completing a painting for a relative. I had worked happily and efficiently on the painting for several days.

Then, for my noontime meditation, I sat in a chair near a window instead of in my regular meditation chair.

Two nights before this dream, I read a new-to-me passage in which the author writes that many people, even mystics, don't realize that there is a stage beyond letting go of waking-life concerns when the meditator can become conscious of "God as Love."

PMID Step 2: Connect your previous day (often the day before) thoughts to your dream to detect which thoughts may have prompted this dream's responses. Write "I thought" statements and record when you thought them.

Last night I thought about a prescription toothpaste I have been using and wondered if it could now be bought over the counter. (Later I found this toothpaste still needs to be prescribed.)

Yesterday I continued to think about the passage I read a couple days ago about "God as Love." I felt deeply inspired from thinking of the word "love" and words "God as love."

PMID Step 3: Select and define major words and phrases from your write-up of this dream to discover the dream's personalized meanings. The general definition for "phrases" as used in this step is "a string of words," which can be phrases, clauses, or whole sentences.

- **Go to a store and ask a favorite clerk for a toothpaste product:** Ties to my pre-dream thoughts on whether the toothpaste I use is now an over-the-counter product.
- **See the clerks as they take relaxing noontime meditations:** This ties to my noontime meditation yesterday.
- **Woman clerk I especially like:** When a person in a dream is other than someone I connect to in waking life, I sometimes consider that person representative of some characteristic of my own. Here I believe the woman clerk I especially like ties to me. The time during which this dream took place was a time when I especially liked myself. As to this dream, having worked happily and efficiently on the painting for a relative is one key for especially liking myself at the time of this dream.
- **Desire for her to be with a child, her child, or perhaps an adult, at least someone she loves, during the noontime meditations:** Yesterday I desired to reach the stage I read about two nights ago, a stage beyond letting go of waking life concerns when the meditator can become conscious of "God as Love."
- **See her sitting in something like a windowsill:** For my noontime meditation yesterday I sat in a chair near a window instead of in my regular meditation chair. Here, again, the dream indicates the woman is me.
- **Isn't with this loved person:** Yesterday I was unsuccessful in reaching the stage of becoming aware of "God as Love."
- **Is smiling and taking time to relax:** The dream shows there are benefits from taking time to relax even without reaching the meditation depth desired.

Solution in This Dream: During the dream when I *do feel pleased for her*, the dream emphasizes fine relaxed emotions can occur from taking time for meditation even without reaching the depth desired.

This next dream is one I woke from, recorded, and then opened my email. In the email was an announcement of a world Solstice Meditation for the same day. Read the dream and interpretations to discover why the timing of the Solstice Meditation was excellent for me.

DREAM: SEND FLOWERS TO TERRORIST LEADER

I am in a class of mature students. There is something about a terrorist leader, but I don't understand I am responsible to do anything about him and so I pay little attention.

Later I am checking my email on the teacher's laptop computer. Her laptop computer is on her travel bag. She asks me about sending flowers to this terrorist, and she names him.

So now I realize I am responsible for arranging to send the flowers. I realize the intention is for our class members to pay for the flowers, and so I ask how much I should collect from each class member. I don't want to ask for a lot from them. The teacher says, "Well, think of the return on the cost, like the better flowers you send the more benefits will be returned."

PMID Step 1: Connect your previous day (often the day before) events to the dream to discover the theme of this dream.

Yesterday, while my husband and I were eating at a fast food place, I couldn't help but hear the TV news that continued on and on about a world terrorist.

PMID Step 2: Connect your previous day (often the day before) thoughts to your dream to detect which thoughts may have prompted this dream's responses. Write "I thought" statements and record when you thought them.

Last night I thought about media's often negative emphases. I wondered if I am one of few people who find negative-news amplifications offensive and unwise.

PMID Step 3: Select and define major words and phrases from your write-up of this dream to discover the dream's personalized meanings. The general definition for "phrases" as used in this step is "a string of words," which can be phrases, clauses, or whole sentences.

- **Mature students:** People who have background experiences to carry out the message of this dream.
- **Teacher:** I am being taught something in this dream.
- **I pay little attention:** In waking life, I tried to turn my thoughts away from the repetitive negative news, and away from the terrorist leader.
- **Checked my email:** After I typed the dream this morning, I opened my email. In the email was an announcement of a world Solstice Meditation for today.
- **Teacher's laptop computer:** This represents communications by way of a computer, email communication.

- **On her travel bag:** Distance communication by way of email, which in retrospect represents the Solstice Meditation announcement email sent during the night and that I opened the morning after this dream.
- **Asks me about sending flowers to this terrorist:** I am asked to do something kind instead of thinking angry thoughts about this terrorist leader and the repetitive newscasts about his activities.
- **Realize I am responsible for arranging to send the flowers**: I am responsible for arranging peacefulness meditation for the terrorist leader during the world Solstice Meditation today.
- **Intention is for our class members to pay for the flowers:** Our class members are other participants in the world Solstice Meditation. When I make my meditation known during the Solstice Meditation, other participants will be influenced to meditate for peacefulness for the terrorist leader.
- **Better flowers you send, the more benefits will be returned:** The more sincere the meditations for him, the greater the benefit that will be returned in some way.

PMID Step 4: Compare your emotions in your dream with your pre-dream, waking-life emotions to discover whether your waking-life emotions accurately reflect how you feel about the issue in this dream.

During my dream, though I feel uncertain about what to do regarding the terrorist leader, I seem to feel calm. Last night I felt upset by the repetitive newscasts about the terrorist leader. As noted before, dreaming emotions are often more accurate than pre-dream waking-life emotions about the issue in the dream.

This dream is a response to my pre-dream thoughts and emotions from the repetitive newscasts about this terrorist leader. The dream shows there is something I can do to relieve the reactions I feel that will likely contribute to world peace in some way: Meditate on peacefulness for the terrorist leader during the world Solstice Meditation. Those meditations will influence others in today's Solstice Meditation to meditate on peacefulness for the terrorist leader. I also take this suggestion as a fine one to continue beyond the Solstice Meditation.

How I've Used This Dream: I participated in the Solstice Meditation during my regular noontime meditation. In my regular noontime meditation I meditate for "Peace and love and oneness and joy and light in the hearts and minds and souls of all the peoples of the world." I name several leaders and countries, some who seem peaceful to me and some who seem other than peaceful to me, but the terrorist and his country were not on my list.

From the time of this dream I have included the terrorist leader and his country in my meditations. Those meditations have given me peace about this leader and his country. Perhaps those meditations contribute to world peace in some way. I am still learning, but just imagine the potential effects on world peace as the number of humans who recognize the Higher Self potential in each human being increases.

As noted above, my regular 20-minute noontime meditation began several years ago. More recently, when I became lax in my dedication to the noontime meditations, my dreaming mind let me know how important those meditations are.

DREAM: CRITICALLY IMPORTANT TO TAKE REGULAR NOONTIME 20-MINUTE MEDITATIONS

I am in our unfamiliar Great Room. It is a long room. I am busy with some kind of activity or project. A man comes to the door at 20 minutes to the hour. I invite him in. He asks about the appointment I have with a woman this morning. It is a regular appointment. I was so engrossed in this work I was doing that I forgot all about it.

The man says, "We will just cancel your signup for the future." I am surprised. No, I don't want to cancel my scheduled times with her. I even thought I could make it in time today. I feel quite surprised this man comes personally to our door, and a bit before the appointment time, to tell me about the appointment. More surprising to me is he just assumes I won't be keeping the appointment today and then even says he will cancel this scheduled activity for the future.

PMID Step 1: Connect your previous day (often the day before) events to the dream to discover the theme of this dream.

Yesterday I didn't take a full 20-minute noontime meditation. Instead I pressed myself to answer email questions.

Last night I became enamored about writings in a small booklet I happened to find two days ago. This is the first time I recalled reading the booklet.

PMID Step 2: Connect your previous day (often the day before) thoughts to your dream to detect which thoughts may have prompted this dream's responses. Write "I thought" statements and record when you thought them.

I neglected to record pre-dream thoughts for this dream.

PMID Step 3: Select and define major words and phrases from your write-up of this dream to discover the dream's personalized meanings.

The general definition for "phrases" as used in this step is "a string of words," which can be phrases, clauses, or whole sentences.

- **Man comes to the door at 20 minutes to the hour:** Twenty minutes and "a bit before the appointment time" are clues that define the appointment as the noontime meditation.
- **Busy with some kind of activity or project:** This ties to yesterday's activity of pressing myself to answer email questions.
- **Asks about the appointment I have with a woman this morning:** The only woman involved in my work yesterday morning was me. At first I thought the dream woman was the one whose writings enamored me the night before this dream, but the time of the man's visit and the time of my intense email work connect more with the noontime meditation.
- **Regular appointment:** I have known from my dreams, and from the relaxation I derive from noontime meditations, that I do need to meditate every noon.
- **I was so engrossed in this work I was doing that I forgot all about it:** This directly connects to my observation: "Yesterday I didn't take a full 20-minute noontime meditation. Instead I pressed myself to answer email questions."
- **Man says, "We will just cancel your signup for the future":** Once I stop noontime meditations, that habit will become established, which will cancel the appointments.
- **Even thought I could make it in time today:** During the dream the man comes to the door at 20 minutes to the hour. At 20 minutes to the hour I was likely thinking I would finish the emails and still take my full noontime meditation.
- **Don't want to cancel my scheduled times with her:** The noontime meditations uplift me, especially from my seeing "peace and love and oneness and joy and light in all the peoples in the world," including myself.

During my dream I am surprised when the man says, "We will just cancel your signup for the future." Yet during my dream "I don't want to cancel my scheduled times with her." This shows I do want to keep my noontime meditation schedule with my wisdom self, my inner self.

Another time my dreams guide me to meditate is after work at 5:30 p.m. This next dream answers my thoughts about whether I need my being-at-rest "beadwork" 5:30 meditations now. Readers, as we said above about noontime meditations, notice that when you establish a productive custom, such as meditation, your dreaming mind can bring you reminders to keep you on track for those appointments.

DREAM: THE 5:30 P.M. BEADWORK CLASS

I seem to be on a new job. Winona (pseudonym) *is the lead secretary. A fellow comes in. He is an applicant for a program, but I am unfamiliar with the sign-in routine.*

Winona takes the fellow with her to sign up for the beadwork class. She has called and they are doing beadwork in the basement it seems. I think it strange the fellow will do beadwork, but then I think everybody who comes in will do some beadwork. I think about it being almost quitting time, but the bead class is still going.

I go to our high school restroom. Lena (pseudonym) *walks with me. Do we have the brochures here? Lena tells me to put him in office equipment. I think that is strange. Then I realize this is the business department. I think she will sign him in.*

There are three packets of brochures at our desks. Applicants do not bring these back.

It is five minutes until quitting time, twenty-five minutes after the hour. I take out my portable typewriter. I plan to take it home. . . .

PMID Step 1: Connect your previous day (often the day before) events to the dream to discover the theme of this dream.

I have been receiving some intuitive insights during my work with dreams. However, my success with the longer after-work meditations has been limited now. So last night I did meditate before I went to sleep about how to still my mind and body in relaxation for meditation. The theme for this dream is my 5:30 after-work meditation.

PMID Step 2: Connect your previous day (often the day before) thoughts to your dream to detect which thoughts may have prompted this dream's responses. Write "I thought" statements and record when you thought them.

For the last several days I thought perhaps this is not a time when I need the longer after-work (5:30 p.m.) meditations because I receive quick insights during my work hours, and during my work with dreams. I wondered if these quick insights during work hours and during work with dreams could replace the after-work meditation now. A thought-question this dream responds to is: "Do the quick insights I receive during my work hours and during my work with dreams replace my need for the after-work 5:30 meditation?"

PMID Step 3: Select and define major words and phrases from your write-up of this dream to discover the dream's personalized meanings. The general definition for "phrases" as used in this step is "a string of words," which can be phrases, clauses, or whole sentences.

- **New job:** Something new for me is represented in this dream.
- **Applicant for a program:** In the context of this dream, the program is my longer after-work (5:30 p.m.) meditations.
- **Am unfamiliar with the sign-in routine:** Here the dream symbolizes my lack of success with the after-work meditation. The reason my success is limited is my own Dream-Guided Meditation Model has become unfamiliar to me! Read on to understand why.
- **Winona:** This person is a very knowledgeable legal secretary. Her presence represents something I need to do according to structured procedure, the structure of the Dream-Guided Meditation Model.
- **Takes the fellow with her to sign up for the beadwork class:** Beadwork for me represents the rosary. Though I don't use rosary beads, they represent meditation for me.
- **Doing beadwork in the basement:** Symbolizes meditation in the depth of the mind, which in the past has happened most for me during the after-work 5:30 meditation.
- **Think it strange the fellow will do beadwork:** Ties to my last night's thoughts on whether I need to continue my longer after-work meditations. Here the dream indicates that I should use my logical reasoning skills to realize the importance of the longer after-work meditations. (I subscribe to the idea that all persons, male and female, have both logical reasoning skills, male, and intuitive feeling skills, female.)
- **Think everybody who comes in will do some beadwork:** Shows while I am wondering whether to continue the after-work meditations, I value taking some meditation time.
- **Think about it being almost quitting time:** It is almost time for my after-work longer meditation.
- **Bead class is still going:** After-work meditation.
- **Go to our high school restroom with Lena:** The restroom symbolizes waste materials that need to be eliminated. Here, I need to let go of thinking the quick insights I receive during my work hours and during my work with dreams will replace my need for the after-work 5:30 meditation. Lena has often struck me as a non-structured person.
- **Lena tells me to put him in office equipment:** This reflects my pre-dream thoughts that my non-structured, quick insights while I work in my office may be all the meditation I need now.
- **Think it strange (that Lena tells me to put him in office equipment):** For me, something strange in a dream usually means I am doing something strange in waking life. It is strange to think my

non-structured, quick insights while I work eliminate my need for longer meditations.

- **Three packets of brochures:** This likely symbolizes the three-stage Dream-Guided Meditation Model given in a dream. "Quiet Your Whole Body, Slow Your Breath, and Still Your Thoughts and Listen to Become Aware of Your Still State."
- **Applicants do not bring these back:** The meditator is expected to keep using the three-stage meditation model every day. Thus, symbolically the meditator keeps the "three packets of brochures."
- **Five minutes until quitting time, twenty-five minutes after the hour:** I assume this is 5:25 p.m., almost 5:30, the time I've stopped work each day for my longer meditation.
- **Portable typewriter:** Portable indicates that I can easily change from taking structured after-work meditation to non-structured, quick insights while I work. Here this represents continuing work during regular meditation time.
- **Plan to take it (portable typewriter) home:** This represents that I plan to continue work past working hours but that is the time to let the work go and meditate.

During my dream I feel at a loss on how to handle signing the fellow in for the beadwork class. Dreams chagrin the dreamer at times. Here the dream shows I overlooked the structure needed for the Dream-Guided Meditation Model.Thus the answer to my pre-dream thought-question on whether the quick insights I receive during my work replace my need for the after-work meditation is: "No." "Continue the end-of-the-workday-at-5:30 structured meditations."

Winona and Lena are my friends from the past. As indicated in my personal meanings of strings of exaçt words from the dream, Winona was a very knowledgeable legal secretary. Her presence represents the fact that there is something I need to do according to a structured procedure. Lena has long struck me as doing things her own way instead of following detailed instructions. Though doing things my own way is often helpful, discontinuation of the structured meditation given to me in the meditation model dream would be unproductive.

Use of This Dream: I studied the structure of the meditation model and continued my after-work 5:30 meditation time. The good news is that quick insights continue during my work hours and during my work with dreams.

Dreams did continue with reminders when I missed my regular after-work meditation. The message of this next dream is to take the longer meditation every day, even when the meditation time is later than usual.

DREAM: DO NOT SKIP MEDITATION TIMES

I am at our medical doctor's unfamiliar office—it seems like it could be in a basement and is a larger place than his actual office. On recall I came because of a physical strain, but when I woke I didn't recall what the pain was. (I wouldn't go to our doctor unless I really had something to go for.)

He has me lie down and he starts talking to me about a woman for whom he did the same procedure he is going to do for me. He talks about her going to a church. The church where she goes could be where he goes. He says she became inspired from his doing this procedure. I am impressed and somewhat surprised because the doctor has not been a person who talks in those terms.

Then the doctor starts to talk quietly to me. In a little bit I realize, "My goodness, this is meditation. He is taking me into meditation." That inspires me, but instead of being still I tell him I know the woman, that she used to go to the church where I go before she changed to this church. I say a couple of other things. Then he says, or somehow I know, he is done treating me and I don't feel inspired, don't feel like the woman felt. I know it is because I kept interrupting the meditation.

I feel awful. I get up to go. I wish I could retreat. I look as he walks away; I want so much to call him back and do this right, but I know the time is over. I feel just awful.

PMID Step 1: Connect your previous day (often the day before) events to the dream to discover the theme of this dream.

My husband and I are moving. We are doing most of the moving ourselves. It is enjoyable work with my husband. However, for several days I haven't taken my regular meditation time at 5:30. Yesterday was one of those days. I did have time and could have taken time because we were home at 7:00; it was late, but I still could have meditated.

Last night I intended to read my favorite book by a spirituality teacher. However, I picked a different book up by mistake. Though the book wasn't the one I meant to read from, I did read a few pages. The pages I read focus on what some people call the dark night of the soul and pain that could come with it. Words stating that the dark night is often painful stuck with me.

PMID Step 2: Connect your previous day (often the day before) thoughts to your dream to detect which thoughts may have prompted this dream's responses. Write "I thought" statements and record when you thought them.

Last night I did think about missing meditation, but I thought, "Well, during the day I thought about projects for what I believe are my missions." I thought, "Well maybe meditation isn't as important when I keep thinking about 'spirituality projects' during the day." The dream's response is a strong caution to keep from missing meditation.

As for what I read regarding the dark night as often being painful, I thought about some rough times I've had and how all is so well with me now. Then I wondered if my current experience is a different kind of dark time.

PMID Step 3: Select and define major words and phrases from your write-up of this dream to discover the dream's personalized meanings. The general definition for "phrases" as used in this step is "a string of words," which can be phrases, clauses, or whole sentences.

- **Our medical doctor:** This connects to my thoughts from my last night's readings about pain that could come with the dark night of the soul. Our medical doctor symbolizes help to relieve thoughts about pain.
- **Seems like it could be in a basement:** This suggests this dream message is from the depths of the mind.
- **Larger place than his actual office:** I have a larger issue than a medical concern. The doctor's help in this dream is to relieve thoughts about pain instead of actual physical pain.
- **Came because of a physical strain on recall, but when I woke I didn't recall what the pain was:** My thoughts about my last night's readings on the dark night of the soul and pain left greater impressions than I realized. Thoughts leave powerful effects on emotions. Meditation can change painful thoughts and related emotions.
- **Starts talking to me about a woman for whom he did the same procedure he is going to do for me:** The same procedure he did for the woman turns out to be meditation. This says to meditate to understand and discover how to relieve painful thoughts and related emotions.
- **Says about her going to a church:** Here I believe the church the woman goes to is the long meditation I usually do, but have skipped during our moving activities.
- **Church:** Though I usually meditate at home, churches symbolize meditation for me.

- **Church where she goes could be where he goes:** The meditation, the longer after-work meditation, is the one the doctor plans to lead for me.
- **Says she became inspired from his doing this procedure:** This indicates inspiration achieved from meditation.
- **I am impressed and somewhat surprised because the doctor has not been a person who talks in those terms:** This dream isn't about a medical condition; it is about relieving thoughts about pain.
- **Realize, "My goodness, this is meditation":** The solution in this dream is to meditate, something I've skipped during our move.
- **Inspires me:** Meditation does inspire me.
- **Used to go to the church where I go:** The "church," the belief I have during our moving activities is: "Well, maybe meditation isn't as important when I keep thinking about 'spirituality projects' during the day."
- **Before she changed to this church:** This indicates the after-work longer meditation.
- **Know he is done treating me and I don't feel inspired, don't feel like the woman felt:** What I did in place of meditation (thinking about "spirituality projects") isn't an inspirational replacement for meditation.
- **Know it is because I kept interrupting the meditation he was doing:** Here I believe the dream gives strong opposition to my having missed meditation during our moving activities.

PMID Step 4: Compare your emotions in your dream with your pre-dream, waking-life emotions to discover whether your waking-life emotions accurately reflect how you feel about the issue in this dream.

The emotions I feel during my dream reflect my true emotions about having given up the longer meditation sessions during our move. During the dream *I feel awful. I get up to go. I wish I could retreat. I look as he walks away and want so much to call him back and do this right, but I know the time is over. I feel just awful.* These are strong revelations of my true emotions about having missed meditation sessions during our move.

Research shows emotions in dreams are often more accurate than the person's waking-life appraisal of his or her emotions about a specific issue. Below is support for the accuracy of dreaming emotions.

The dreaming mind exaggerates. A major area of dreaming exaggeration is emotions. Emotions in dreams are, however, intrinsically honest, even while being exaggerated. This honesty is noteworthy because it means

> that dreams can tell us when our waking-life appraisals of emotions are inaccurate. (Duesbury, 2010, p. 85)

Jung (1966) claimed that the intrinsic honesty of emotional content in dreams helps dreamers set their dreams within recent emotional experiences and, consequently, helps people apply their dreams to their waking lives.

Wolman and Ullman (1986) contend that the dreaming mind is often a more accurate reflection of the person's emotions than the person outwardly expresses or knows.

Hmmm. I slipped up again and missed the 5:30 meditation time. Read this next dream and personalized meanings to realize I could have symbolically stopped work and meditated at the regular time even though we were traveling on vacation. The term the dream uses for stopping work is "take the work car home." As these dreams illustrate, there is a strong work orientation in my nature.

DREAM: LATE FOR 5:30 CHOIR PRACTICE—OH, THE WORK CAR STARTS

I plan to go to choir practice at my childhood church. I have Mr. Delsing's (pseudonym) *work car plus our car. There is a shorter way to go, but the way I am going is the longer way.*

There is snow on the road; the road is a ledge or rim-like narrow road. We go around the rim, and the narrow road ends.

It is 5:30 or 6:30, time for choir practice to start. I think I will go anyway though I will be late. What shall I do with Mr. Delsing's work car, though? I have keys to the work car. I get in and turn the keys. It starts! I feel surprised.

Then Paul (pseudonym) *is here. I wonder if he could drive Mr. Delsing's work car back home. I ask what else he has to do. Then I see Paul in his business clothes and I know he really doesn't have time to drive Mr. Delsing's work car home.*

Our car I am driving is a white car, a large white car.

> **PMID Step 1:** Connect your previous day (often the day before) events to the dream to discover the theme of this dream.
>
> Yesterday we traveled in the country and came to a road that just ended. Most times now I take the suggestions in my *5:30 Beadwork Class* dream, and I do take my regular 5:30 meditation time. Yesterday, though, we were not back at our lodging place by 5:30.
>
> **PMID Step 2:** Connect your previous day (often the day before) thoughts to your dream to detect which thoughts may have prompted

this dream's responses. Write "I thought" statements and record when you thought them.

I have no recorded account of my pre-dream thoughts for this dream, but see my definitions below. I must have thought about meditating when we were still traveling at 5:30.

PMID Step 3: Select and define major words and phrases from your write-up of this dream to discover the dream's personalized meanings. The general definition for "phrases" as used in this step is "a string of words," which can be phrases, clauses, or whole sentences.

- **Plan to go to choir practice:** The choir represents music. As shown in other dreams in this book, music symbolizes inner calm during meditation, the still state. Here the attempt to get to choir practice shows I do plan to meditate this day.
- **Childhood church:** From early childhood the meaning of churches for me has been a place to worship. After I learned about meditation, my dreams began to include churches as symbols for meditation.
- **Cars:** Often represent the body, the vehicle that carries us around.
- **Shorter way to go:** I could have quieted my body away from being in a work mode.
- **Way I am going is the longer way:** The longer way here means my body was not quieted in preparation for meditation. See below: "Work car starts" symbolizes I was in a work mode.
- **Snow on the road:** This represents coldness in my nature when I was unprepared for quiet meditation yesterday.
- **Narrow road ends:** This connects the dream to our daytime experience of the road ending. The end of the road symbolizes a time to turn around, and turn my attention to quieting my body for meditation.
- **5:30 or 6:30:** My usual meditation time is 5:30. An hour difference reflects the time zone difference between where we are vacationing and our home at the time of this dream.
- **Mr. Delsing's work car:** Mr. Delsing has a car he only drives for work. Here his work car represents the work mode of my body during my regular meditation time.
- **Work car starts**: This symbolizes that I was in a work mode. The work car, my body, was not in a quiet state in preparation for meditation.
- **Paul:** An industrious person who is often at work on some project. In this dream Paul represents my work orientation.
- **Car I am driving is a white car, a large white car:** The Delsings have a second car, a large white car they use for their relaxation activities. White suggests spirituality to me. Symbolically, I was "driving" myself toward meditation and I could have relaxed into

meditating while we were traveling. That would have been the shorter route to meditation. (Note: In waking life my husband was driving.)

During my dream I feel surprised the work car starts, in other words surprised my body is still in a work mode even though I planned to meditate. I don't have records of emotions I felt yesterday when my body was not in a relaxed state during my regular meditation time.

A relationship in this dream is mine to Paul. The characteristic I most associate with Paul is his work ethic. He rarely slows down, rarely takes breaks from his work. My reaction to his work ethic, admiration most times, helps me understand his role in this dream.

How I'm Using This Dream: I use this dream as a reminder to concentrate on relaxation during my regular meditation time whether I am in my regular meditation place or not.

The next dream is another helpful dream, though it made me feel terrible during and after the dream. This time my worried thoughts interfered with successful after-work meditations.

DREAM: DEVASTATED—MY COACH DOESN'T ASK ME TO BE ON THE TEAM

I learn my high school basketball coach is going to have special basketball practices. The special practice is at 5:30. I think of that time as after school.

My coach hasn't asked me to come to the special practices yet. I finally ask one of the team members, one on the first team. She tells me they have been practicing for four days already.

I feel awful. I wonder who is playing in my place, but I do not ask. She, or someone else, tells me my coach is doing the extra practice because he is planning to win over a team she names.

I feel so, so bad.

Then I am on a bus that my coach is driving. I decide to ask him why he didn't invite me to be on the team. He is solemn and obviously in a moody temperament. He says I was going with a known criminal, or perhaps he said a person who did criminal acts. I try to think who that is, who he could be referring to. And he says I was meandering in the hallway. In my mind's eye, I see the second-floor hallway of the high school where I went to school. I repeat the word "meandering" and I ask, "Meandering?" He repeats something about meandering in the hallway. I see in my mind's eye the sauntering back and forth and still I don't know when I did that.

So I tell him I feel the worst I have ever felt, just feel terrible. He doesn't soften.

Then I tell him the other side. I tell him how great it was when he put me on the team. However, some people are talking loud so it is hard for me to make myself heard over the noise.

When I woke I felt tremendous relief it was a dream; it seemed so real. Then as I wrote the dream down in my notebook, I again felt terrible that I had messed up in some way.

PMID Step 1: Connect your previous day (often the day before) events to the dream to discover the theme of this dream.

An event from last night that connects to this dream is my husband and I talked about my school basketball coach and the difference in my life because of having been selected to join the first team.

I haven't been having relaxed meditation while we are traveling on vacation. (Readers, note I'd already had dream guidance that shows I could have "relaxed into meditating while we were traveling" in *Late for 5:30 Choir Practice—Oh, the Work Car Starts*.)

PMID Step 2: Connect your previous day (often the day before) thoughts to your dream to detect which thoughts may have prompted this dream's responses. Write "I thought" statements and record when you thought them.

Yesterday during my attempts at deep meditation, my mind wandered into worried thoughts. A thought-question this dream may respond to is: "Do worried thoughts interfere with successful meditation?"

PMID Step 3: Select and define major words and phrases from your write-up of this dream to discover the dream's personalized meanings. The general definition for "phrases" as used in this step is "a string of words," which can be phrases, clauses, or whole sentences.

- **My school basketball coach:** A person dedicated to coaching his team to doing well and winning.
- **Special practice is 5:30:** My regular after-work meditation time.
- **Coach hasn't asked me to come to the special practices yet:** We are traveling on a vacation trip west. Though I did attempt to meditate yesterday, I was unsuccessful in relaxing into deep meditation.
- **Have been practicing for four days already:** This could be the number of days I've missed relaxing into dedicated meditation.
- **Coach is doing the extra practice:** The extra practice here means extra practice needed to quiet my mind of the worried thoughts I had yesterday when I tried to meditate.
- **Because he is planning to win:** Here "win" means to overcome worried thoughts that interfere with meditation.

- **Going with a known criminal:** I broke the Universal Law by thinking negatively yesterday.
- **He says I was meandering in the hallway:** These are my meandering thoughts though I had planned to be in a quiet state all through the day.
- **In my mind's eye, I see the second-floor hallway of the high school where I went to school:** This is symbolic of higher thoughts, but meandering negative thoughts interfered.

PMID Step 4: Compare your emotions in your dream with your pre-dream, waking-life emotions to discover whether your waking-life emotions accurately reflect how you feel about the issue in this dream.

During the dream I feel the worst I have ever felt. I just feel terrible for being left off the team. Here the dream shows my worried thoughts were far more devastating to successful meditation than I realized in waking life before this dream.

PMID Step 5: Explore your dream for possible solutions to problems, including changing (or affirming) your thoughts, attitudes, or behaviors.

This dream answers whether worried thoughts interfere with meditations: Yes, they do. Successful meditation requires intense dedication and practice to still the thoughts and listen to become aware of the still state.

PMID Step 6: Explore your dream for family and other relationships shown or implicated in the dream.

The prominent relationship in this dream is my basketball coach from many years ago. He was a fine coach who guided us to winning records. My recall of the intense dedication with which he coached helps me recognize my lack of dedication to meditation at the time of this dream.

How I Used This Dream: The day after this dream I focused on my inner still state most of the day. I came into a deep loving feeling. That night I had the dream offered below, which reflects success from focusing on my inner still state.

DREAM: WISE WOMAN RECOGNIZES MY SPIRITUALITY LEANINGS

I am at some place, could be a university or school of some kind. . . . Then I am sort of floating around, for want of better description.

There is a full-bodied, well-kept woman studying—reading a book—a ways from where I am. I wonder whether I should visit with her or not—I do not want to interfere with her studying. However, I sort of automatically float to her or somehow end up right beside her.

I feel like my very common self. The woman seems upper level to me. She shuts her book and talks with me. She says to me," I know you are a mystic." I am surprised she can notice that.

PMID Step 1: Connect your previous day (often the day before) events to the dream to discover the theme of this dream.

After yesterday's dream, *Devastated—My Coach Doesn't Ask Me to Be on the Team*, I spent much of the day focusing on my inner still state. I had my books handy to read but decided I could do okay without them. A theme these events connote is The Power of Dedicated Focused Attention on the Inner Still State.

PMID Step 2: Connect your previous day (often the day before) thoughts to your dream to detect which thoughts may have prompted this dream's responses. Write "I thought" statements and record when you thought them.

Yesterday I had my books handy to read but decided I could do okay without them. One thought-question this dream responds to is: "Should I have read the books I had handy instead of focusing on my inner still state?"

Last night I wondered if I would have a dream about yesterday's success. Another thought-question that arises is: "Is this dream a response to my success from focusing on my inner still state most of yesterday?"

PMID Step 3: Select and define major words and phrases from your write-up of this dream to discover the dream's personalized meanings. The general definition for "phrases" as used in this step is "a string of words," which can be phrases, clauses, or whole sentences.

- **I am at a university or school of some kind:** I am being taught something of academic significance.
- **Floating around, for want of a better description:** This is a symbolic description of my wandering thoughts yesterday regarding how important it would have been to read a book.
- **Full-bodied, well-kept woman studying—reading a book—a ways from where I am:** Ties to yesterday's thoughts about the books I had handy. (Though my stature is different from this woman's stature. I am a slender woman.)
- **Wonder whether I should visit with her or not:** This again ties to my thoughts about the books I had handy yesterday and my quandary about reading them instead of focusing on my inner still state most of the day.
- **Feel like my very common self:** Even after success with deep meditation and coming into deep loving feelings, I still returned to feeling

like my very common self after those experiences. It seems to me this is normal. At least that is how it has been for me.

- **Woman seems upper level to me:** This could really be an "upper-level" dream woman come to answer my pre-dream thought-question.
- **Shuts her book and talks with me:** This answers my pre-dream thought-question: "Should I have read the books I had handy yesterday instead of focusing on my inner still state?" Here this act indicates deep meditation in the silence brought results greater than reading books would have brought me.
- **"Know you are a mystic":** I believe this reflects my pre-dream thought-question: "Is this dream a response to my success from focusing on my inner still state most of yesterday?" The answer, I believe, is: Yes.

Another "when to meditate" time is during life's transitions, as the next dreams reflect. The first two dreams take me to my high school gymnasium, as does the dream that brought the Dream-Guided Meditation Model. Recall that, during the meditation model dream, Mr. Sampson *walks with me to the . . . gymnasium at the school I attended during grade and high school.*

DREAM: THERE IS A VOICE

As I sleep the words seem to come in my dream: "There is a voice. . . ." I'm carrying something sort of awkward to carry, books, in a plastic bag, perhaps in my arms. I am going to the bleachers in my high school gymnasium to look for someone there.

PMID Step 1: Connect your previous day (often the day before) events to the dream to discover the theme of this dream.

I woke during the night and listened for what I've called the Inner Voice. Then I fell back to sleep and dreamed this dream.

This dream occurred during the final week of my associate professor of accounting work. (I resigned a few months ago.) Today is a new psychology class in which I am enrolled.

PMID Step 2: Connect your previous day (often the day before) thoughts to your dream to detect which thoughts may have prompted this dream's responses. Write "I thought" statements and record when you thought them.

I thought about today's new psychology course and about this being the last week I will teach accounting.

PMID Step 3: Select and define major words and phrases from your write-up of this dream to discover the dream's personalized meanings. The general definition for "phrases" as used in this step is "a string of words," which can be phrases, clauses, or whole sentences.

- **There is a voice:** This, I believe represents an intuitive knowing.
- **Carrying something sort of awkward to carry, books, in a plastic bag:** I am mindful of the psychology course I will begin the day of this dream. "Sort of awkward to carry" symbolizes the surprisingly dispirited emotions I felt about the transition to being a student again.
- **Going to the bleachers:** This is a place to sit and watch instead of playing the game, which seems to indicate the role of a student.
- **In my high school gymnasium:** Symbolic of a transition in my life. Selection to the high school basketball team was a significant life change for me. I'd never even seen a real basketball game before. Dedication, I believe, was the reason I was a successful member of the team.
- **Looking for someone there:** This indicates that I am looking for inspiration for how to handle the transition, the difference between teaching accounting to studying psychology.

PMID Step 4: Compare your emotions in your dream with your pre-dream, waking-life emotions to discover whether your waking-life emotions accurately reflect how you feel about the issue in this dream.

During this dream my emotions as symbolized by the books that were "sort of awkward to carry" coincides with the surprisingly dispirited emotions I felt about the transition to being a student again before this dream. Though I looked forward to today's new psychology class, I felt a bit dispirited. When emotions in the dream and waking-life pre-dream emotions coincide, this indicates that the dreamer's pre-dream appraisal of emotions was accurate.

How This Dream Directs the Transition: In my view, the reason I was selected to the high school basketball first team when I'd never even seen a real basketball game before was the dedication I had for playing basketball. This indicates that the way to transition from my teaching career to being a student is to dedicate myself in the same manner as when I learned to play basketball.

Two years after the *There is a Voice* dream I transitioned from periodic psychology courses to full-time student for a counselor education MS degree. Then a dream took me back to times when I graded CPA exams to help me make that transition.

DREAM: STAY WITH THE STYLE LEARNED WHILE GRADING CPA (CERTIFIED PUBLIC ACCOUNTANT) EXAMS

I am at work. We are all sitting in rows to do the work. I have been doing personal stuff while I work. . . .

Then the others all stop working. I think they are stopping early. I need to get more CPA exams graded. I look at the clock. It is 5:30. Oh, my goodness, I wonder if I have graded enough exams to keep up with the quota. However, it is too late today to grade any more papers.

PMID Step 1: Connect your previous day (often the day before) events to the dream to discover the theme of this dream.

I've been having difficulty becoming still, though I realize I need to still my thoughts at other times, not only during meditation.

PMID Step 2: Connect your previous day (often the day before) thoughts to your dream to detect which thoughts may have prompted this dream's responses. Write "I thought" statements and record when you thought them.

Yesterday I thought about activities I will do after counselor education courses I'm enrolled in begin. Yet, I still thought I will stop at 5:30 for meditation, which poses a thought-question for this dream: "Will my counselor education coursework leave time for meditation?"

PMID Step 3: Select and define major words and phrases from your write-up of this dream to discover the dream's personalized meanings. The general definition for "phrases" as used in this step is "a string of words," which can be phrases, clauses, or whole sentences.

- **All sitting in rows to do the work:** A classroom of rows during the counselor education courses I will take, the courses I thought about last night.
- **Have been doing some personal stuff while I work:** Doing some personal stuff while I work connects to the later part of this dream about grading CPA exams.
- **Others all stop work:** Ties to yesterday's thoughts about my 5:30 meditations after my counselor education classes begin.
- **Think they are stopping early:** As happened the day before this dream, it was after my regular 5:30 meditation time before I stopped work. Here the dream reflects my pre-dream concern on whether I'll stop my study in time for my regular 5:30 meditation time after the counselor education courses begin.
- **I need to get more CPA exams graded:** During my periodic trips to grade CPA exams, I attended spirituality services where I learned

about meditation. It was then that I began noontime meditations, after-work meditations, and maintaining a meditative state while I graded exams. Maintaining a meditative state helped me exceed the quota of exams we were expected to grade each day.

- **It is 5:30:** My regular after-work meditation time.
- **Wonder if I have graded enough exams to keep up with the quota:** This again pulls from my experiences of grading CPA exams, and ties to yesterday's thoughts about how much time the counselor education coursework will take.
- **Too late today to grade any more papers:** This answers my pre-dream thought-question, "Will my counselor education coursework leave time for meditation?" The answer is yes *when* I do as I did while grading CPA exams: maintain a meditative state during the course work in the same manner as when I graded CPA exams. Then my study will go efficiently and thus will leave time for my regular meditations.

When I enrolled as a full-time student for a counselor education degree, I resigned from my position of associate professor of accounting, which left writing as my only work. At the time I was unaware that this transition would affect my appreciation for my work as a writer. This next dream encourages me to expand my mind to other computer drives (vast reaches of the human mind) to again realize the value of my dream-guided writings. Computers symbolize the mind for me because of their abundant capacities.

DREAM: EXPAND THE MIND TO "OTHER DRIVES" DURING MEDITATION

I am at my computer, which is at the side of my desk in the lobby of the first floor of the university building that houses my former office. The dean's secretary comes by. She puts her computer disc into my computer. She doesn't even ask me if she can use my computer, nor does she talk to me; but I don't mind or complain because I have a lowly position.

The dean's secretary is checking the drives with her disc. I notice she checks from one drive to another . . . G, H . . . I only work in the A drive. I wonder if I know how to get my computer back to the A drive.

I don't work very hard and I don't have very important tasks in this lower position. When I was in an upper-level position, others treated me with respect, but now I'm not in a highly respected position.

Then I am involved in doing my laundry here. Gee, my nightgown is in with my work clothes. I must work long hours when I even wear my nightgown here at work.

PMID Step 1: Connect your previous day (often the day before) events to the dream to discover the theme of this dream.

I recently resigned from teaching accounting.

Last night I seemed close to becoming aware of the still state, but those feelings passed on by.

PMID Step 2: Connect your previous day (often the day before) thoughts to your dream to detect which thoughts may have prompted this dream's responses. Write "I thought" statements and record when you thought them.

Last night when I lacked success in becoming aware of the still state of Stage Three, I wondered what I needed to do.

PMID Step 3: Select and define major words and phrases from your write-up of this dream to discover the dream's personalized meanings. The general definition for "phrases" as used in this step is "a string of words," which can be phrases, clauses, or whole sentences.

- **My computer . . . at the side of my desk:** In the context of this dream, my mind.
- **University building that houses my former office:** I recently resigned from teaching at this university.
- **Dean's secretary. . . . Puts her computer disc into my computer:** In this dream the secretary's computer disc symbolizes the far reaches of the mind. At the time of this dream, the dean's secretary has computers with more capacity than those the faculty members have in their offices.
- **Checking the drives with her disc:** This is a response to my pre-dream thoughts about the still state stage that is in the Dream-Guided Meditation Model. Here, checking the drives symbolizes checking whether I have ability to clear my thoughts and listen to become aware of my still state.
- **Checks from one drive to another . . . G, H:** Symbolic of the vast reaches of the human mind and indicates I do have the ability (space) to access the vast reaches of the mind.
- **Only work in the A drive:** The A drive represents the limited scope of my meditations when I do not become aware of my still state. "The A: and B: drives are leftovers in Windows from the days when a floppy drive was standard issue and required for software installations" (Humphries, 2011).
- **Wonder if I know how to get my computer back to the A drive:** This connects to my recent experiences, especially the previous night when I seemed to be becoming aware of my still state.

- **Don't work very hard:** The dream chagrins me by showing I haven't been working very hard with my meditations.
- **Don't have very important tasks in this lower position:** Here the dream shows the transition away from my teaching role has left me considering my work with writing, my only work at the time of this dream, as a lower position.
- **Must work long hours when I even wear my nightgown here at work:** Nightgowns are the attire when I, the dreamer, receive dream-guided material for my writing.

The prominent person in this dream is the dean's secretary. My earlier experiences with her resourcefulness help me understand her high-level role in this dream.

How to Use This Dream: Change my conception of being a writer as a lower position than my former position of teaching. Change from being lax with my writing to realizing I do have the ability (space) to access the vast reaches of my mind for my meditations and for the work ahead of me as a writer.

Though most dreams in this chapter show specific times or specific occasions to meditate, the next two dreams show the still state is within us all the time. We could practice meditation at any time, which for purposes of this book is a form of mindfulness. "For purposes of this book, mindfulness is maintaining a meditative state as we go about our daily activities" (Introduction, p. 1).

The next dream uses the terminology "God (Infinite Mind) is talking all the time." The second dream uses the terminology "No matter where you are the leader of the band can track you" to show the inner still state is available all the time.

DREAM: GOD (INFINITE MIND) IS TALKING ALL THE TIME

There is a tall slender male teacher. I only listen to the beginning and to the end of his talk, but he is talking all the time.

PMID Step 1: Connect your previous day (often the day before) events to the dream to discover the theme of this dream.

The night before this dream I read words to this effect: "God is talking all the time."

PMID Step 2: Connect your previous day (often the day before) thoughts to your dream to detect which thoughts may have prompted this dream's responses. Write "I thought" statements and record when you thought them.

The night before this dream, after I read those words, I concentrated on thinking the same phrase: "God is talking all the time."

PMID Step 3: Select and define major words and phrases from your write-up of this dream to discover the dream's personalized meanings. The general definition for "phrases" as used in this step is "a string of words," which can be phrases, clauses, or whole sentences.

- **Tall slender male teacher:** A tall slender man may symbolize the inner teacher in me. I am a tall slender woman with a longtime respect for male teachers. This dream could be saying, "It is logical that the inner still state is available all the time."
- **Only listen to the beginning and to the end of his talk:** Reflects my minute meditations. At the time of this dream I often pause for a minute on the hour and meditate. Then I go back to my regular mental reasoning mode until the beginning of the next hour when I pause and listen again.
- **Talking all the time:** Here this assertion means I could meditate any time day or night. Our access to our inner still state is available all the time.

Several years after the above *God (Infinite Mind) Is Talking All the Time* dream a similar meaning came in another dream. That dream uses music, as do other dreams in this book, as symbolism for having become aware of the inner still state.

DREAM: THERE IS NO PLACE WHERE THE MUSIC PROFESSOR IS NOT

There is a sort of informal music group here. They are professionals, though. There are probably around eight to ten members. I am helping with the setup here in this place where I live. . . . During our setup, someone talks about my musicianship. Somehow they think I have talents in music. . . . One man who is playing in the band is a professor of music here in our local area. . . .

Then it is later and I am in a different place, staying at a motel or hotel. I am talking to someone about this group of musicians.

Then I put in a telephone call to them [the band]. *Surprisingly, a man answers and says my name. He laughs and says they have this "system" (not the right word, but the closest I recall) that no matter where you are they can track you—something like that. This is the man who is the professor of music in our local area. I am surprised he is with the band at this different location.*

PMID Step 1: Connect your previous day (often the day before) events to the dream to discover the theme of this dream.

Last night was another time I read material on the idea there is no place where God (Infinite Mind) is not.

PMID Step 2: Connect your previous day (often the day before) thoughts to your dream to detect which thoughts may have prompted this dream's responses. Write "I thought" statements and record when you thought them.

Yesterday I thought about the limited number of years I have left to live. Those thoughts led me to feeling limited and discouraged and then to thoughts of things I could do to keep inspired.

PMID Step 3: Select and define major words and phrases from your write-up of this dream to discover the dream's personalized meanings. The general definition for "phrases" as used in this step is "a string of words," which can be phrases, clauses, or whole sentences.

- **Sort of informal music group here:** Music in my dreams often symbolizes the abilities to achieve peacefulness of body and mind and become aware of the inner still state. See the several dreams in this book that use music as symbolism for deep meditations.
- **Helping with the setup here in this place where I live:** This is a response to my pre-dream thoughts on the idea there is no place where God is not, and to my thoughts about the limited time we live, and then how to keep inspired. The dream shows how to "set up" answers to those thoughts.
- **During our setup someone talks about my musicianship:** This is a reference to my ability to become aware of the inner still state.
- **Somehow they think I have talents in music:** I must have more talent for becoming aware of the inner still state than I have realized.
- **Then it is later and I am in a different place, staying at a motel or hotel:** The scene changes to show the everywhere-presence of the inner still state.
- **Put in a telephone call to them (the band):** This shows my attempt to contact this something within, this inner capacity.
- **Says they have this "system" (not the right word, but the closest I recall) that no matter where you are they can track you:** In the context of this dream, this is a reference to the ever-present inner still state.

PMID Step 4: Compare your emotions in your dream with your pre-dream, waking-life emotions to discover whether your waking-life emotions accurately reflect how you feel about the issue in this dream.

During my dream I feel surprised *the professor of music in our local area* is with the band at this different location. In the context of this dream, I am surprised there is an ever-present inner ability to become aware of the inner still state.

PMID Step 5: Explore your dream for possible solutions to problems, including changing (or affirming) your thoughts, attitudes, or behaviors.

This dream answers last night's thought-question on how to keep inspired. Keep inspired by realizing the ever-present inner still state, which in this book is a form of mindfulness.

Summary of Chapter 6

Specific times this chapter suggests to meditate are short meditations before work each day, twenty-minute noontime meditations, and longer meditations at the end of the workday. Life's transitions are other times to meditate. Finally, other times are any times we feel inspired to do so. This chapter presents a dream answer to a pre-dream thought-question on how to keep inspired. Keep inspired by realizing the ever-present inner still state. That is, we can practice mindfulness any time. "For purposes of this book, mindfulness is maintaining a meditative state as we go about our daily activities" (Introduction, p. 1).

References

Duesbury, E. M. (2010). *The counselor's guide for facilitating the interpretation of dreams: Family and other relationship systems perspectives*. New York: Routledge.

Humphries, M. (2011). What are the Windows A: and B: drives used for? Retrieved May 12, 2015 from www.geek.com/geek-pick/what-are-the-windows-a-and-b-drives-used-for-1305216/.

Jung, C. G. (1966). *Two essays on analytical psychology*. (R. F. C. Hull, Trans.). Princeton, NJ: Bollingen Series/Princeton University Press.

Wolman, B. B., & Ullman, M. (1986). *Handbook of states of consciousness*. New York: Van Nostrand Reinhold.

7 Where to Meditate

Where to meditate is, of course, up to the preferences of individual meditator. Those preferences can differ according to time, type, and number of meditations for each day or evening. For the 10-minute before-work meditation and for the 20-minute noontime meditation, I usually sit in a rocking chair in my office. Then for the after-work 5:30 meditation I usually lie down in a quiet room in our home.

Other choices people make depend on whether they want to meditate alone or with others, and what their activities are for the day. Some people prefer to meditate with others at work, in churches, or in other public places.

Some people find the deepest meditative quietness in their own homes. For instance, one night after being particularly struck by allegorical words about meditation during the day, I had an open-door dream.

DREAM: OPEN DOOR

Our front door is open a few inches and I see smoke curling up. It is not a fire, though, and I am not afraid. It is dusky.

At the time of this dream I study my dreams and meditate to discover my true place in life. In those ventures yesterday I read some allegorical words about meditation. Smoke was used as symbolic of results from intense inner concentration on the soul. I felt drawn to the teachings, though they were strange for me.

Meanings I developed from major dream phrases and symbols from my write-up of this dream are:

- **Our front door is open a few inches:** The dream shows a productive place for meditation is right where we live. I can meditate right where we live, where I live.

- **See smoke curling up:** This ties to yesterday's readings about smoke as symbolic of results from intense inner concentration on the soul. Intense inner concentration reminds me of the third stage of the Dream-Guided Meditation Model, Still Your Thoughts and Listen to Become Aware of Your Still State.
- **Not a fire, though:** This shows the smoke is a symbol; it isn't an actual fire.
- **Dusky:** There is something in this dream that I do not see, do not understand.

During my dream, *I am not afraid.* In waking life before the dream I gladly accepted the writer's definition of smoke rising as symbolic of a result of intense inner concentration on the soul. My dreaming mind assures me these teachings are safe to follow.

In the context of my day-before impression of the allegorical words about meditation, the Open Door dream means: "Right where we live. I can meditate right where we are, where I am." In response to my pre-dream desire to "strive to discover my true place in life," the dream shows my true place in life is right where we live, in our home.

Some people relax best in nature settings. For instance, the Relaxing Noontime Meditations dream discussed earlier in this book shows a woman (who I believe symbolizes me) leaving her work area and sitting in *something like a windowsill* as she takes a relaxing noontime break. The day before that dream I meditated near my office window, a window that opens out on a nature scene.

Some people are most quieted in the spirituality settings of various religious traditions. For instance, one night I dreamed about being with the people of one denomination with whom I felt at ease and peaceful; the next night I dreamed I stopped at a different denomination's place of worship to meditate before going to work.

Some people like to symbolically go to foreign countries when they meditate, as the next dream shows. It had never occurred to me in waking life that I could picture myself in a foreign country to meditate.

DREAM: CAN PICTURE MYSELF IN A FOREIGN COUNTRY CHURCH AND MEDITATE THERE

I am sitting in a congregation in a church. Seems more I see myself sitting here instead of feeling I am here. This is a church where I feel very much where I want to be; but I think of the church being in the next town, so

I will not go often. Then somehow I realize I can go often. I feel quite good about this.

PMID Step 1: Connect your previous day (often the day before) events to the dream to discover the theme of this dream.

Last night I read the back cover of a book by a leader who teaches about meditation. The back cover shows the leader is in a foreign country. I knew that, but in reading his biography, I realized anew, "Yes, he is leading meditation now in this foreign country." I also read a passage in the book that dreams aren't part of the meditation practices this leader presents. I had also realized that before, but I had resisted dwelling on it.

PMID Step 2: Connect your previous day (often the day before) thoughts to your dream to detect which thoughts may have prompted this dream's responses. Write "I thought" statements and record when you thought them.

Last night after reading the passage that dreams aren't part of the meditation practices this leader presents, I thought again about my meditations as guided by dreams. Then I thought, "No, I don't go this way then." Then later I thought, "But the leader may have yet to notice dream help." (I did not work with dreams when I first started to meditate.) A possible thought-question this dream responds to is: "Do I go the way the leader in the foreign country teaches?"

PMID Step 3: Select and define major words and phrases from your write-up of this dream to discover the dream's personalized meanings. The general definition for "phrases" as used in this step is "a string of words," which can be phrases, clauses, or whole sentences.

- **Sitting in a congregation:** In the context of this dream, this is the leader's congregation I thought about last night.
- **Seems more I see myself sitting here instead of feeling I am here:** The dream suggests picturing myself in the leader's congregation as if I am there in person. This counters last night's first thought, "No, I don't go this way then" and shows me that, yes, I can sit in this church; I do go this way.
- **This is a church where I feel very much where I want to be:** The meditation practices this leader presents are ones that have inspired me for several years.
- **Church being in the next town, so I will not go often:** Being in the next town, in the context of my yesterday's readings and thoughts, symbolizes a foreign country.

- **Then somehow I realize I can go often:** I can often picture myself as being in the teacher's congregation.

PMID Step 4: Compare your emotions in your dream with your pre-dream, waking-life emotions to discover whether your waking-life emotions accurately reflect how you feel about the issue in this dream.

During my dream I feel quite good about being in the foreign country church. In waking life it had never occurred to me I could picture myself where this leader presides and feel I am there.

PMID Step 5: Explore your dream for possible solutions to problems, including changing (or affirming) your thoughts, attitudes, or behaviors.

This dream confirms the meditation practices this leader presents are ones for me to follow. It shows I can picture myself in the leader's congregation as if I am there in person. What a wonderful confirmation dream. I feel most grateful.

How I'm Using This Dream: During meditation times I periodically picture myself in this leader's congregation while I sit quietly in the back and meditate.

Summary of Chapter 7

This chapter details various places for meditation, places that vary according to the meditator's preferences. Among those preferences are at home, in nature settings, at work with others, in churches and other kinds of public places, and even in a foreign country when the meditator pictures being there. For instance, one night after reading teachings I especially like, yet never thinking I could visit the teacher's congregation, in a dream *I realize I can go often*. Because of this dream I periodically picture being in this sanctuary as I meditate.

Conclusion

This book concludes with an uplifting waking-life, pre-dream inner knowing supported by a dream response. The dream came one night after my husband and I attended a university presentation on ice drilling research at the South Pole. When we returned home I thought about the vast, vast, vast parts of the world and worlds beyond that we know absolutely nothing about. I thought, "How can we even know there is God?" I meditated for help. "Please, please help." Then suddenly, still in waking life, I unexplainably felt enormously uplifted; I knew there is Infinite Mind—that this is beyond all tangible things. That night I had a responding dream.

DREAM: RESPONSE TO MEDITATION—UNEXPLAINABLY FELT ENORMOUSLY UPLIFTED; KNEW THERE IS INFINITE MIND—BEYOND ALL TANGIBLE THINGS

There is a man who plays fine music. He has played for this woman's program before, but he isn't playing here now. Then he comes back and plays, but now there is another man who somehow accompanies him. Either I do not want or the man who plays fine music does not want this other man to accompany the fine music; it takes away from the fine musician's presentation. It seems somehow we do persuade the man who played fine music to play again and somehow keep this other man from accompanying the fine music. I feel humbly grateful.

Personalized meanings of the strings of words—phrases, clauses and whole sentences—are:

- **Man who plays fine music:** The power I call Infinite Mind who in my perception is beyond human understanding but is within our experiences. Experiences that convince me are deep meditations and nighttime dreams.

- **Has played for this woman's program before:** In the context of this dream, I believe *this woman* refers to me. *This woman's program* represents times when I have realized human beings have direct access to guidance beyond words and thoughts.
- **Isn't playing here now:** This comes from last night when I thought, "How can we even know there is God?" Reveals I had gone away from realizing humans have direct access to guidance from beyond words and thoughts.
- **Comes back and plays, but now there is another man who somehow accompanies him:** This shows the double belief system I have developed.
- **Either I do not want or the man who plays fine music does not want this other man to accompany the fine music; it takes away from the fine musician's presentations:** When I have a double belief system, one from a tangible god out there, it takes away from my knowing there is Infinite Mind—that this is beyond all tangible things.
- **Somehow we do persuade the man who plays fine music to play again and somehow keep this other man from accompanying the fine music:** This dream scene symbolizes the answer that came during meditation last night: I knew there is a power I call Infinite Mind, that this is beyond all tangible things.

During the dream I feel humbly grateful when the *man who played fine music* plays again. In waking life before this dream I first felt let down and then enormously uplifted when this knowing fell into my mind: I knew there is Infinite Mind—that this is beyond all tangible things.

This dream is a confirmation of last night's sudden and enormously uplifted feelings and knowing in waking life. Then the dream adds wisdom of its own: My question, "How can we even know there is God?" reveals I had reverted to thinking of a tangible god out there. The answer to my question is we *can* know there is Infinite Power when we stop thinking of a tangible god.

Summary of Lessons Presented in This Book

A compilation of the solutions and suggestions for each dream in this book is used to summarize the lessons presented. As you study these lessons may you find helpful ideas for your meditative life. Watch your nighttime dreams for which lessons are helpful for you.

Lesson One: Dreams and meditations are interactive; both are resourceful.
Dream: Dream Work and Inner Work Flow Together

Lesson Two: The three basic stages in the Dream-Guided Meditation Model are Quiet
Your Body, Slow Your Breath, and Still Your Thoughts and Listen to Become Aware of Your Still State with the potential result over time of becoming aware of your Higher Self presence within your being, a presence in all human beings.
Dream: A Meditation Model Given in a Dream

Lesson Three: For the Dream-Guided Meditation Model it is important to quiet the whole body instead of only quieting from the spine up. Quieting only from the spine up leaves no roots.
Dream: Use the Full Tree for Meditation

Lesson Four: When you wake during the night and feel restless, meditate; but meditate in extreme quiet.
Dream: The Teacher Sits in Extreme Quiet for Meditation

Lesson Five: Slow your breath, and it doesn't matter whether the breaths are even or unevenly spaced.
Dream: Play the Metronome Slowly and Uneven Beats Are Okay

Vital Tip: Benefits accrue from these first two meditation stages (Quiet Your Whole Body and Slow Your Breath) without going further. They relax the meditator for the day ahead.

Lesson Six: At least some of the time, even an instant, still your thoughts.
Dream: The Monkey Mind

Lesson Seven: Calmly affirm that thoughts and emotions, especially negative thoughts and negative emotions, are shut out from interfering with your meditations and with your dreams. Usher the dominant thoughts and emotions out first.
Dream: Usher the Dominant Woman and the Others out of the Church

Lesson Eight: Be patient as you wait for your thoughts to clear for deep meditation.
Dream: Responses from Becoming Especially Aware of the Difficulty to Still the Thoughts That Cross the Mind

Lesson Nine: Stand still, be still, still your thoughts.
Dream: Stand Still Is the One Message the Students Understand

Lesson Ten: Recognize effects when you let your thoughts pass by, much like waiting for a train to pass by at a crossing.
Dream: Stand Still and Let the Train of Thoughts Pass By

Lesson Eleven: Attempts to meditate without having practiced and without listening is like expecting to play beautiful music when you haven't practiced.
Dream: Listening and Practice Are Essential for Successful Meditation

Lesson Twelve: For times when it seems you are meditating more on an outer level instead of an inward level, return to studying the Dream-Guided Meditation Model.
Dream: Reminded to Meditate with the Full Dream-Guided Meditation Model

Lesson Thirteen: A reminder to the dreamer-meditator: Use the meditation model, "Quiet Your Whole Body, Slow Your Breath, and Become Aware of Your Still State."
Dream: To Access Deeper Levels during Meditation, Use the Dream-Guided Meditation Model

Lesson Fourteen: Stay with the meditation process and wait patiently! Patient waiting is paramount for successful meditation.
Dream: Stay in the Meditative State and Wait Patiently!

Lesson Fifteen: Keep from becoming drawn into frustrated emotions and a measure of successful meditation will occur.
Dream: Confidence That Yesterday's Second Meditation Was Deep Though Could Have Been Deeper

Lesson Sixteen: During your busiest days it is especially important to take time for meditation to calm yourself. This dream counsels me that meditation would have been symbolically worth $1,000 in calm wisdom for completing my yesterday's work.
Dream: Take Time for Meditation: It Is Worth $1,000 in Calm Wisdom

Lesson Seventeen: It takes intense dedication to go beyond mental awareness to consciousness of the "Fourth Square," the Higher Self potential present within each human being.
Dream: Dedicated Student Causes Me to Say More Than I'd Planned (Infinite Mind and mind are the same. Infinite Mind is the Fourth Square)

Lesson Eighteen: To become conscious of the Higher Self potential within, one must still the mind for insights beyond logical reasoning, beyond words and conscious thoughts.
Dream: Higher Self Consciousness Is Beyond Words and Thoughts

Lesson Nineteen: One of the times to meditate is each morning before going to work.
Dream: Meditate for Guidance Every Morning

Lesson Twenty: Noontime is another time for regular meditations. This dream confirms there are still benefits from meditation without reaching the meditation depth desired.
Dream: Relaxing Noontime Meditations

Lesson Twenty-One: There is something you can do about disturbing events: Meditate for the person and or groups whose actions upset you.
Dream: Send Flowers to Terrorist Leader

Lesson Twenty-Two: When you become uplifted and relaxed from noontime meditations, keep on with that practice. Otherwise dreams may show those

meditation appointments cancelled, which means you have lost, at least for the time, the uplift and relaxation from regular noontime meditations.
Dream: Critically Important to Take Regular Noontime 20-Minute Meditations

Lesson Twenty-Three: Another time to meditate is after work. Study the structured three stages of the meditation model to succeed with after-work meditation.
Dream: The 5:30 p.m. Beadwork Class

Lesson Twenty-Four: Dreams can bring strong revelations of distress from missing regular meditations.
Dream: Do Not Skip Meditation Times

Lesson Twenty-Five: It isn't necessary to be in your regular meditation place to relax during your regular meditation times.
Dream: Late for 5:30 Choir Practice—Oh, the Work Car Starts

Lesson Twenty-Six: Dedication and practice are necessary to become aware of your still state.
Dream: Devastated—My Coach Doesn't Ask Me to Be on the Team

Lesson Twenty-Seven: There is power in dedicated focused attention on the still state.
Dream: Wise Woman Recognizes My Spirituality Leanings

Lesson Twenty-Eight: Another "when to meditate" time is during life's transitions.
Dream: There Is a Voice

Lesson Twenty-Nine: During transition times, be in a meditative state during your work, not only during specific meditation times.
Dream: Stay with the Style Learned While Grading CPA (Certified Public Accountant) Exams

Lesson Thirty: During work transitions expand your confidence by meditating: Meditate by realizing the vast reaches of your mind.
Dream: Expand the Mind to "Other Drives" during Meditation

Lesson Thirty-One: We could practice mindfulness any time day or night. Access to our still state is available all the time.
Dream: God (Infinite Mind) Is Talking All the Time

Lesson Thirty-Two: Keep inspired by realizing the ever-present still state.
Dream: There Is No Place Where the Music Professor Is Not

Lesson Thirty-Three: I can meditate right where I am. In response to my pre-dream desire to "strive to discover my true place in life," the dream shows my true place in life is right where we live, in our home.
Dream: Open Door

Lesson Thirty-Four: It is possible to picture yourself in meditation in an inspiring leader's congregation even when the leader teaches in a foreign country.
Dream: Can Picture Myself in a Foreign Country Church and Meditate There

Lesson Thirty-Five: Waking-life responses to meditation can be confirmed by subsequent dreams, and added wisdom can be included in the subsequent dreams.
Dream: Response to Meditation—Unexplainably Felt Enormously Uplifted; Knew There Is Infinite Mind—Beyond All Tangible Things

Appendix A One Hundred Year Turn of the Twenty-First Century Coincidence

One hundred years after Freud published *The Interpretation of Dreams* (1900), another award-winning dream interpretation model came into being. Freud purposely waited until the turn of the twentieth century to publish his book. I, Evelyn M. Duesbury, fully intended 1999 to be the year my dream interpretation model would be accepted for my counselor education master degree thesis. By coincidence, it was the turn of the twenty-first century, 2000, when the thesis was accepted.

What happened? During 1999 I prepared a story-form thesis with seven series of relationship dreams interpreted by the case study participant who used my Personalized Method for Interpreting Dreams (PMID) model. I found a published story-form thesis for support. The thesis committee rejected my story-form thesis.

When I finally completed a traditional research format that met the committee's requirements, it was 2000. Gratefully, the standard research format (Problem, Review of Literature, Methodology, Results, Summary, Discussions, and Conclusions) resulted in the thesis being selected as the University of Wisconsin-Whitewater thesis of the year in 2000.

Then in 2011 it occurred to me, "My goodness, my thesis was at the turn of a century." Then I wrote a history of the PMID model and included the above paragraphs. One night after editing my history of the model, I had a responding dream.

DREAM: ONE HUNDRED YEAR TURN OF THE CENTURY COINCIDENCE (OCTOBER 16, 2011)

I see 100 packages of toilet tissue all neatly stacked in rows on a shelf. I am impressed.

PMID Step 1: Connect your previous day (often the day before) event(s) to the dream to discover the theme of this dream. The events may appear in either symbolic or literal terms in your dream. Write down the appropriate events and record when they occurred.

Last night I edited the history of the PMID model I had written. Prominent in the history is the coincidence of the model being published 100 years after Freud's *The Interpretation Of Dreams*. Thus the theme of this dream is simply the one hundred year turn of the century coincidence.

PMID Step 2: Connect your previous day (often the day before) thoughts to your dream to detect which thoughts may have prompted this dream's responses and provide thought-questions that this dream responds to. Similar to events, your thoughts may appear in your dream in either symbolic or literal terms. Write "I thought" statements and record when you thought them.

Last night I thought about whether my history of the PMID model is now in final form. This dream responds to that thought-question.

PMID Step 3: Select and define major words and phrases from your write-up of this dream to discover the personalized meanings of the dream. Consider effects of day-before-your-dream events, thoughts, and earlier experiences on the meaning of each major dream phrase and symbol. The general definition for phrases as used in this step is "a string of words," which can be phrases, clauses, or whole sentences.

- **The number 100:** In the context of this dream, this represents the turn of the twenty-first century when the Personalized Method for Interpreting Dreams (PMID) came into being.
- **Packages of toilet tissue:** "Toilet paper, a usually soft absorbent paper … used for cleaning the body after defecating or urinating" (Encarta Webster College Dictionary, 2005). From facilitating other's use of the PMID model and from using the PMID model with my own dreams, I know a common personal meaning of toilet tissue is the need to eliminate waste (stress) from strained reactions during relationship experiences. Elimination of stress from reactions during relationship experiences connects to the full PMID model, including Step 6, which addresses relationship systems perspectives.

PMID Step 4: Compare your emotions in your dream with your pre-dream, waking-life emotions to discover whether your waking-life emotions accurately reflect how you feel about the issue in this dream. Note that the issue may be a relationship issue. What differences, if any, do you find between your emotions in your dream and your waking-life emotions? It is useful to periodically review your emotions in your dreams about the main issue or relationship.

During my dream I am impressed with the 100 packages of toilet tissue all neatly stacked in rows on a shelf. In waking life before this dream, I felt hesitant about whether to publish the history of the PMID model. Emotions in dreams, though often exaggerated, are intrinsically more accurate than our waking-life appraisal of emotions about the issue at hand. Here my dreaming emotions show I am confident enough to publish the turn of the century coincidence of the PMID model coming into being.

PMID Step 5: Explore your dream for possible solutions to problems or for changing (or affirming) your thoughts, attitudes, or behaviors. Consider your responses to each PMID model step, including Step 6, as you search for solutions and suggestions in this dream. Give primary attention to the power of your before-your-dream thoughts (PMID Step 2) to act as questions that your dream answers.

In response to my thoughts about whether my history of the PMID model with emphases on it being a turn of a century model is now in its final form, the dream answers that thought-question by showing *100 packages of toilet tissue all neatly stacked in rows on a shelf.* All neatly stacked in rows on a shelf indicates this is a well-written narrative.

There is one more step in the PMID model. Step 6 asks the dreamer to explore the dream for family and other relationship systems perspectives to discover whether the dream reflects reactions during earlier experiences with family or other major relationships. Though there are no relationships identified in this dream, Step 6 is where the dreamer records his or her reactions shown in the dream being interpreted. The dreamer's interpretation of a series of dreams about a particular relationship often gradually alleviates the dreamer's stressful reactions.

With the PMID model, the dreamer works alone or with a counselor. As the dreamer changes his or her reactions to others, the system gradually changes with no need to approach others. This is the systems perspective.

After first offering a book for publication that includes the One Hundred Year Turn of the Century Coincidence, we decided that book is best kept for personal use. Though I've written other books, none have seemed appropriate for inclusion of the One Hundred Year Turn of the Century Coincidence.

A Dream-Guided Meditation Model and the Personalized Method for Interpreting Dreams is an appropriate book for this news: Publication of the award-winning Personalized Method For Interpreting Dreams (PMID) one hundred years after Freud's model adds to readers' confidence in the PMID model.

Reference

Encarta Webster's College Dictionary. (2nd ed.). (2005). New York: Bloombury.

Appendix B Caveat on Bad or Worrisome Dreams

Edward Bruce Bynum, Ph.D.

By now, you have become aware that dreams and working with your own dreams can be powerful catalysts for understanding the deeper dynamics and realities of your emotional life, especially as it flows into the important parts of the lives of those for whom we feel love, anger, jealousy, kinship, rivalry, pain, and joy within our most important moments. While these moments of insight and feeling usually have a grounding and satisfying effect, we must also be aware that they can be disturbing at times on an intimate level.

When this occurs, it is important to consider exploring these feelings with others. It may even be useful at times to consult a professional counselor. Although not usual, this need does occur even with normal but highly stressful dreams. An example would be a dream series in which we wake up frightened or alarmed by what seems to occur repeatedly. This may be around an incident, trauma, or tragedy that befell you or the family member. It may be about what seems to be a memory or fragment of a memory of something that is trying to come to the surface. It is important in these situations to remember that a dream may be emotionally true but not factually true. A dream may present a symbolic situation to you rather than an actual lived moment or series of past situations.

The unconscious is the great treasure house of not only our loves, hopes, and expectations but also our primal fears, anxieties, and social-cultural traumas that have not actually physically occurred to us but rather have impacted us on a psychological level. All the painful images painted each night on the nightly news of prisoner abuse, degradation, and torture give rise to a bottomless ocean of negative counter-images in our collective dreams. Therefore, when you have negative and fearful dreams that repeat themselves, dreams in which you awaken repeatedly in a panic, or dreams in which there is a sickening sensation and a sense of foreboding and dread that follows you through the day, consider speaking with a professional counselor who is well versed in these intimate matters (Duesbury, 2007, pp. 66–67).

Reference

Duesbury, E. M. (2007). *Living dreams, living life: A practical guide to understanding your dreams and how they can change your waking life.* Canada: Trafford and Amazon Kindle.

Index

For Product Safety Concerns and Information please contact our EU representative GPSR@taylorandfrancis.com
Taylor & Francis Verlag GmbH, Kaufingerstraße 24, 80331 München, Germany

www.ingramcontent.com/pod-product-compliance
Ingram Content Group UK Ltd.
Pitfield, Milton Keynes, MK11 3LW, UK
UKHW022157190926
475702UK00003B/77

* 9 7 8 1 1 3 8 6 9 3 3 3 3 *